Dr. Birdley Teaches Science!

Introducing Cells

Featuring the Comic Strip

Middle and High School

Innovative Resources for the Science Classroom

Written and Illustrated by Nevin Katz

Incentive Publications, Inc.

Nashville, Tennessee

About the Author

Nevin Katz is a teacher and curriculum developer who lives in Amherst, Massachusetts with his wife Melissa and son Jeremy.

Nevin majored in Biology at Swarthmore College and went on to earn his Master's in Education at the Harvard Graduate School of Education. He began developing curriculum as a student teacher in Roxbury, Massachusetts.

"Mr. Katz" has been teaching science over 6 years, in grades 6 through 11. He currently teaches Biology, Environmental Science, and Physical Science at Ludlow High School in Ludlow, Massachusetts.

Nevin's journey with Dr. Birdley and the cast began in the summer of 2002, when he started authoring the cartoon and using it in his science classes. From there, he developed the cartoon strip, characters, and curriculum materials. After designing and implementing the materials, he decided to develop them further and organize them into a series of books.

Cover by Geoffrey Brittingham

Edited by Jill Norris and Carolyn Lowe

ISBN 978-0-86530-530-0

1   2   3   4   5   6   7   8   9   10   10   09   08   07

PRINTED IN THE UNITED STATES OF AMERICA
www.incentivepublications.com

TABLE OF CONTENTS

Educational Objectives

Central Goals: • To introduce cells and explain why they are the smallest units of life
• To discuss major types of cells, discuss how they were discovered, and introduce the cell theory

Unit	Primary Objective(s)	Standard
1. Why Cells?	1. Define cells and explain their importance. 2. Provide examples of how cells give living things form and function.	1, 4
2. The Hierarchy of Life	3. Explain that cells combine to form tissues, organs, and systems. 4. Identify eight levels of organization in multicellular living things.	1, 4, 5
3. The Smallest Units of Life	5. Explain why the cell is the smallest unit of life. 6. Relate cells to organelles, molecules, and atoms.	1, 7
4. Characteristics of Living Things	7. Define six characteristics of life. 8. Provide examples of how cells demonstrate them.	2, 3
5. The Amoeba	9. Show that cells are alive by illustrating life processes performed by the amoeba, a one-celled organism.	2
6. Discovering Cells	15. Explain the role of the microscope in discovering cells. 16. Introduce the contributions of Hooke and Leeuwenhoek.	3
7. The Cell Theory	17. Introduce the three major statements of the cell theory. 18. Explain the reasoning and evidence behind each statement.	

FIND OUT WHICH CHAPTERS MATCH YOUR LESSON GOALS!

National Frameworks

This page matches the relevant national frameworks with the units in this book.

National Science Content Standards, Grades 5-8:
Structure and Function of Living Systems, Regulation and Behavior, and Scientific Inquiry

1. All organisms are composed of cells – the fundamental unit of life. Most organisms are single cells; other organisms, including humans, are multicellular. (Units 1, 2, 3, 5, and Review Unit)

2. Cells carry on the many functions needed to sustain life. They grow and divide, thereby producing more cells. This requires that they take in nutrients, which they use to provide energy for the work that cells do and to make the materials that a cell or an organism needs. (Units 4 and 5)

3. Specialized cells perform specialized functions in multicellular organisms. (Unit 6)

4. Groups of specialized cells cooperate to form a tissue, such as a muscle. Different tissues are in turn grouped together to form larger functional units, called organs. (Units 1 and 2)

5. Each type of cell, tissue, and organ has a distinct structure and set of functions that serve the organism as a whole. (Units 2, 6, and Review Unit)

6. Current scientific knowledge and understanding guide scientific investigations. (Review Unit)

7. Scientific explanations emphasize evidence, have logically consistent arguments, and use scientific principles, models, and theories. (Units 3 and Review Unit)

8. All organisms must be able to obtain and use resources, grow, reproduce, and maintain stable internal conditions while living in a constantly changing external environment. (Unit 4)

National Academies Press, 2005
http://www.nap.edu/readingroom/books/nses/

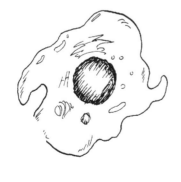

Dr. Birdley Teaches Science – Introducing Cells

Overview of Introducing Cells Source Cartoons

The difficulty level ranges from easy (L1) to very challenging (L3).

Cartoon	Central Focus	Challenge Level	Related Topics
Why Cells? *page 15*	Significance of Cells	L1	Tissues, Organs, Systems
Know Your Levels *page 25*	Hierarchy of Life	L2	Introduction to Cells
Thw Hierarchy of Life *page 30*	Hierarchy of Life	L2	Introduction to Cells
The Smallest Units of Life *page 35*	Cells, Organelles, Molecules, Atoms	L2	Levels of Organization
The Wisdom of Don *page 36*	Cell Reproduction & Growth	L1	Cell Division
Life on the Web *page 45*	Six Characteristics of Life	L1	Cell Division, Membrane
Interview with a Cell *page 46*	How Cells Show Characteristics of Life	L2	Discussion of what life is
The Amoeba *page 57*	Unicellular Organisms	L2	Cell Division, Mitosis
Cell Size *page 67*	Role of the Microscope in the Discovery of Cells	L1	History of Science, Metric Units
Hooked on Cells *page 68*	Robert Hooke, Who Discovered Cells	L1	Cell Walls
A Small World *page 76*	Antony Van Leeuwenhoek, Who Discovered Microbes	L1	Microbes
The Cell Theory *page 81*	The Three Major Statements of the Cell Theory	L1	Hierarchy of Life Cell Reproduction

Dr. Birdley Teaches Science – Introducing Cells

TEACHER'S GUIDE

Contents

THE SOURCE CARTOON

GREETINGS! MY NAME IS DR. BIRDLEY. I AM HERE TO EXPLAIN WHAT THIS BOOK IS ALL ABOUT.

AT FIRST GLANCE, THIS LOOKS LIKE A BOOK OF ENTERTAINING CARTOONS...

WITH HANDSOME CHARACTERS SUCH AS MYSELF.

BUT UPON FURTHER INSPECTION...

EGADS! THESE CARTOONS ARE EDUCATIONAL!

PRECISELY.

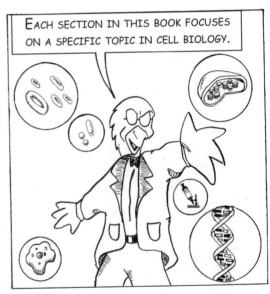

EACH SECTION IN THIS BOOK FOCUSES ON A SPECIFIC TOPIC IN CELL BIOLOGY.

EACH CARTOON COMES WITH A SET OF RELATED ASSIGNMENTS.

THEY CAN BE USED FOR LESSON TIME,

GROUP ACTIVITIES,

OR DRAMATIC READINGS.

FOLLOW ME, AND I WILL SHOW YOU HOW TO USE THEM!

KATZ '04

Dr. Birdley Teaches Science – Introducing Cells

The Source Cartoon

The *Source Cartoon* explains the central concepts of the unit. It is usually one or two pages in length. Expect to find the following in a source cartoon:

• A central idea with supporting details

• Visual images related to the topic being presented

• Explanations of science concepts

• Several characters who explain the information to each other or to the reader

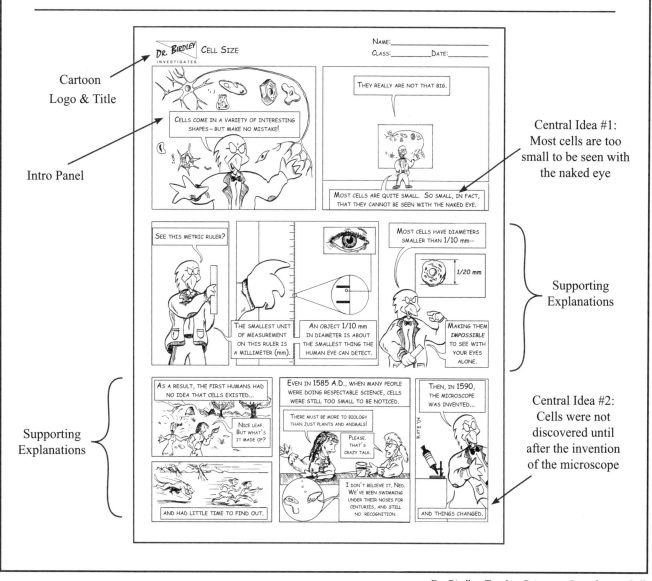

Cartoon Logo & Title

Intro Panel

Supporting Explanations

Central Idea #1: Most cells are too small to be seen with the naked eye

Supporting Explanations

Central Idea #2: Cells were not discovered until after the invention of the microscope

The Cartoon Profile

The *Cartoon Profile,* which outlines a source cartoon's science content, is useful for planning or teaching a lesson. Central elements include:
- the cartoon's objectives,
- vocabulary
- main ideas
- related national standards.

The "questions for discussion" below the image, are useful for getting students engaged and checking for understanding.

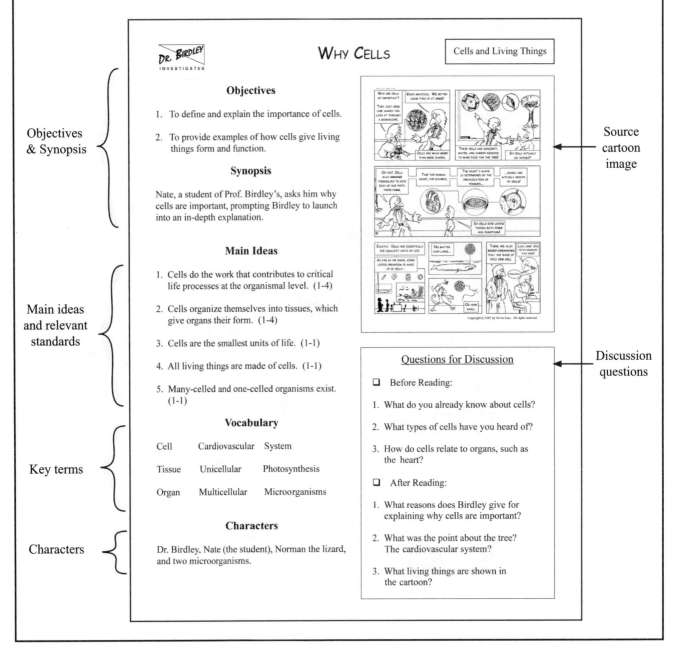

Assignments & Assessments

While a chapter's assignments help students build comprehension, quizzes can assess students' knowledge of key points from a given chapter. Examples of five major assignments and one quiz are pictured below.

Study Questions

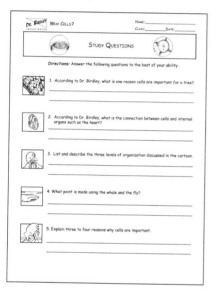

Visual Exercise

Graphic Organizer

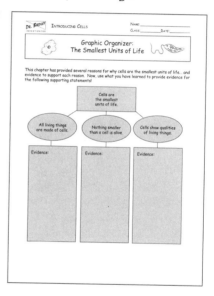

Vocabulary Build-up

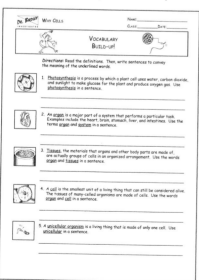

Background Article

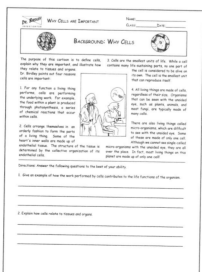

Quiz

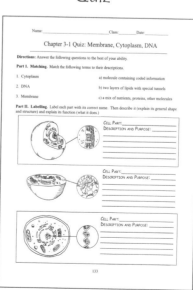

Dr. Birdley Teaches Science – Introducing Cells

Cell Unit: Day 1

AH! THERE YOU ARE.

YOU'RE IN LUCK! I'M ABOUT TO TEACH A LESSON INVOLVING A CARTOON AND ITS RELATED ASSIGNMENTS.

PreLesson: List four questions you have about cells.

Objectives: To discuss the importance of cells.

To introduce four levels of organization in living things.

THIS IS WHAT MY MAIN BOARD LOOKS LIKE BEFORE A LESSON.

Vocabulary:
cell
tissue
organ
system
multicellular
unicellular

AGENDA
1. PreLesson
2. Vocab Build-up
3. Read Cartoon
4. Discuss it
5. Study Questions
6. Visual Exercise
7. Lab Activity

HERE I HAVE COPIES OF THE CARTOON AND ASSIGNMENTS...

AS WELL AS THE EQUIPMENT FOR THE LAB ACTIVITY.

I CARRY THIS CLIPBOARD DURING THE LESSON.

IT CONTAINS THE CARTOON PROFILE AND COPIES OF THE HANDOUTS.

TO SEE THE RELATED EXERCISES, PROCEED TO THE NEXT PAGE!

KATZ '05

Dr. Birdley Teaches Science – Introducing Cells

Sample Lesson Plan

This sample lesson plan integrates materials from Unit 1 as a means of introducing cells. The overall format shown below can be applied to a range of different lessons.

Lesson Objective: To define cells and explain their significance

A. ***Warm-up:*** Students list what they already know and questions they have.

B. ***Sharing ideas:*** The teacher reviews the warm-up with students to learn about their prior knowledge.

C. ***Vocabulary:*** Students complete the vocabulary build-up, using key words in sentences.

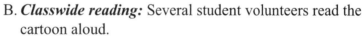

A. ***Introducing the Cartoon:*** The teacher leads a discussion on the *Before Reading* questions from the cartoon profile.

B. ***Classwide reading:*** Several student volunteers read the cartoon aloud.

C. ***Discussion:*** The teacher leads a discussion on the *After Reading* questions from the cartoon profile.

D. ***Reading in pairs:*** Students read again in pairs, highlighting key words and writing comments on a separate sheet of paper.

A. ***Independent Practice:*** Students complete supplementary assignments from unit 1, which include:
- study questions
- visual exercise
- background section questions
- graphic organizer
- Unit 1 quiz

Periodically, the class reviews the answers to the exercises.

B. ***Activity:*** Students examine cell types under a microscope using different magnifications. They then draw each specimen.

As the four volunteers read the cartoon aloud, the audience listens and circles key words.

Dr. Birdley Teaches Science – Introducing Cells

A HANDS-ON ACTIVITY

Dr. Birdley Teaches Science – Introducing Cells

Unit 1: Why Cells Are Important

Contents

NAME:_____

CLASS:_____ DATE:_____

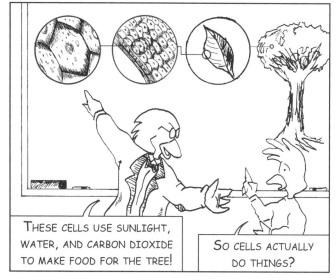

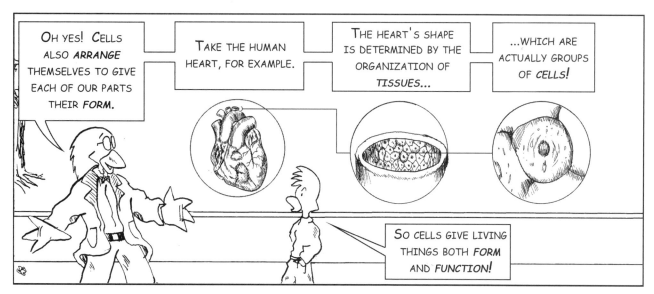

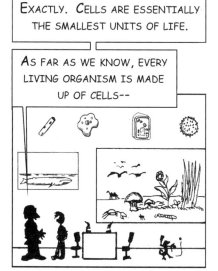

Dr. Birdley Teaches Science – Introducing Cells

WHY CELLS?

Cells and Living Things

Objectives

1. To define and explain the importance of cells.

2. To provide examples of how cells give living things form and function.

Synopsis

Nate, a student of Dr. Birdley's, asks him why cells are important, prompting Birdley to launch into an in-depth explanation.

Main Ideas

1. Cells do the work that contributes to critical life processes at the organismal level.

2. Cells organize themselves into tissues, which give organs their form.

3. Cells are the smallest units of life.

4. All living things are made of cells.

5. Many-celled and one-celled organisms exist.

Vocabulary

cell	cardiovascular	system
tissue	unicellular	photosynthesis
organ	multicellular	microorganisms

Characters

Dr. Birdley, Nate (the student), Norman the lizard, and two microorganisms

Questions for Discussion

Before Reading:

1. What do you already know about cells?

2. What types of cells have you heard of?

3. How do cells relate to organs, such as the heart?

After Reading:

1. What reasons does Birdley give for explaining why cells are important?

2. What was the point about the tree? The cardiovascular system?

3. What living things are shown in the cartoon?

Dr. Birdley Teaches Science – Introducing Cells

BACKGROUND: WHY CELLS?

The purpose of this cartoon is to define cells, explain why they are important, and illustrate how they relate to tissues and organs. Dr. Birdley points out four reasons cells are important:

1. For any function a living thing performs, cells are performing the underlying work. For example, the food within a plant is produced through photosynthesis, a series of chemical reactions that occur within cells.

2. Cells arrange themselves in an orderly fashion to form the parts of a living thing. Some of the heart's inner walls are made up of endothelial tissue. The structure of the tissue is determined by the collective organization of its endothelial cells.

3. Cells are the smallest units of life. While a cell contains many life-sustaining parts, no one part of the cell is considered to be alive on its own. The cell is the smallest unit that can reproduce itself.

4. All living things are made of cells, regardless of their size. Organisms that can be seen with the unaided eye, such as plants, animals, and most fungi, are typically made of many cells.

There are also living things called microorganisms, which are difficult to see with the unaided eye. Some of these are made of only one cell. Although we cannot see single-celled microorganisms with the unaided eye, they are all over the place. In fact, most living things on this planet are made up of only one cell!

Directions: Answer the following questions to the best of your ability.

1. Give an example of how the work performed by cells contributes to the life functions of the organism.

_____

_____

_____

2. Explain how cells relate to tissues and organs.

_____

_____

_____

Dr. Birdley Teaches Science – Introducing Cells

WHY CELLS?

NAME:_____

CLASS:_____DATE:_____

STUDY QUESTIONS

Directions: Answer the following questions to the best of your ability.

1. According to Dr. Birdley, what is one reason cells are important for a tree?

_____

_____

2. According to Dr. Birdley, what is the connection between cells and internal organs such as the heart?

_____

_____

3. List and describe the three levels of organization discussed in the cartoon.

_____

_____

4. What point is made using the whale and the fly?

_____

_____

5. Explain three to four reasons why cells are important.

_____

_____

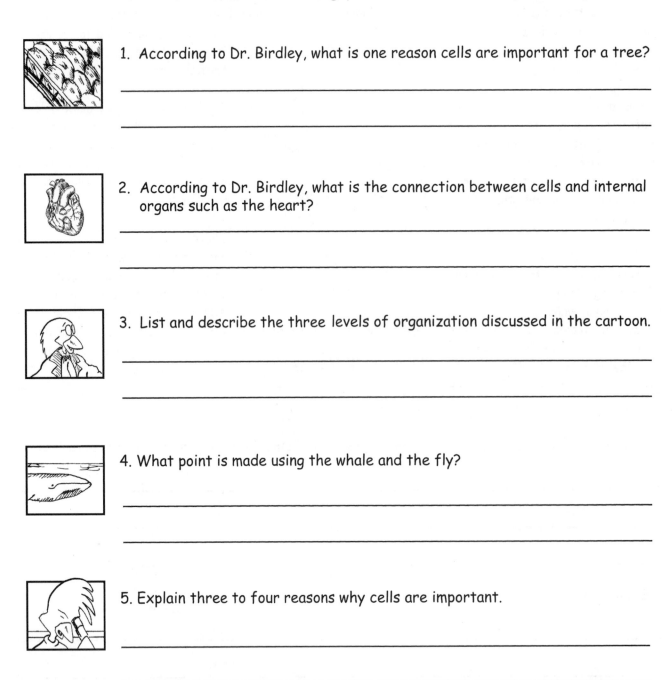

Dr. Birdley Teaches Science – Introducing Cells

TISSUES OF THE HEART

The heart is made of four major types of tissues. Learn about them by filling in the missing words.

Use the word bank!

KATZ '04

WORD BANK

HEART BEAT	CELLS
PROTECTION	FUNCTIONS
STRUCTURE	CONTRACTIONS
COMMUNICATE	CONTROL
LINING	SUPPORT

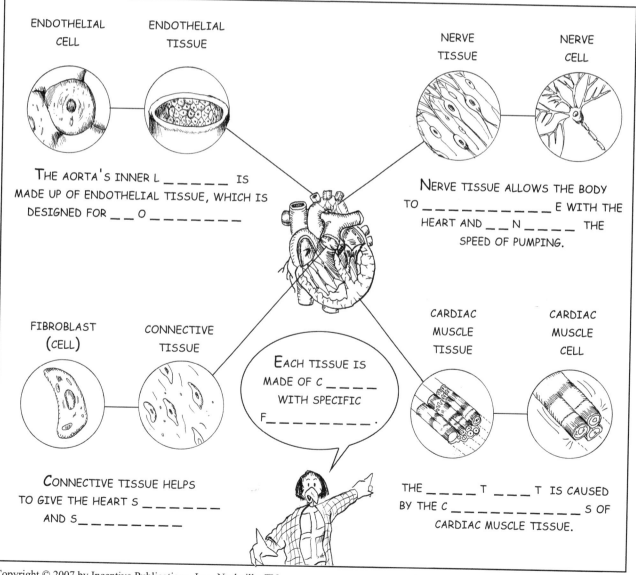

ENDOTHELIAL CELL   ENDOTHELIAL TISSUE

NERVE TISSUE   NERVE CELL

THE AORTA'S INNER L _ _ _ _ _ _ IS MADE UP OF ENDOTHELIAL TISSUE, WHICH IS DESIGNED FOR _ _ O _ _ _ _ _ _ _

NERVE TISSUE ALLOWS THE BODY TO _ _ _ _ _ _ _ _ _ _ E WITH THE HEART AND _ _ N _ _ _ _ THE SPEED OF PUMPING.

FIBROBLAST (CELL)   CONNECTIVE TISSUE

EACH TISSUE IS MADE OF C _ _ _ _ _ WITH SPECIFIC F _ _ _ _ _ _ _ _ _ .

CARDIAC MUSCLE TISSUE   CARDIAC MUSCLE CELL

CONNECTIVE TISSUE HELPS TO GIVE THE HEART S _ _ _ _ _ _ _ AND S _ _ _ _ _ _ _ _

THE _ _ _ _ T _ _ _ T IS CAUSED BY THE C _ _ _ _ _ _ _ _ _ _ _ S OF CARDIAC MUSCLE TISSUE.

Dr. Birdley Teaches Science – Introducing Cells

DR. BIRDLEY INVESTIGATES
PLANT CELLS & PHOTOSYNTHESIS

NAME:_____

CLASS:_____ DATE:_____

LABEL EACH PART OF THE DIAGRAM WITH THE APPROPRIATE TERM. USE THE WORD BANK!

– KATZ '05 –

WORD BANK

CHLOROPLAST	SUNLIGHT
CARBON DIOXIDE	PLANT
WATER	CELL
OXYGEN GAS	PHOTOSYNTHESIS
FORMATION OF GLUCOSE	

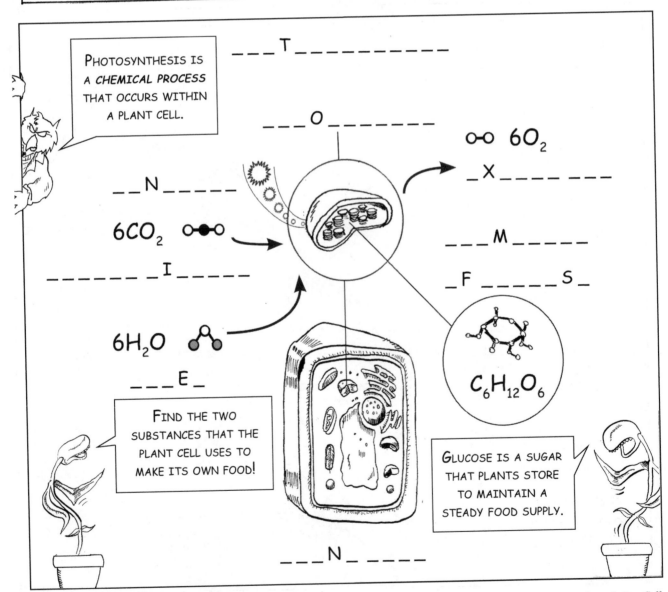

PHOTOSYNTHESIS IS A **CHEMICAL PROCESS** THAT OCCURS WITHIN A PLANT CELL.

_ _ _ T _ _ _ _ _ _ _ _ _ _

_ _ _ O _ _ _ _ _ _ _ _

_ _ N _ _ _ _ _ _

$6CO_2$

_ _ _ _ _ _ _ _ _I _ _ _ _ _ _

$6H_2O$

_ _ _ E _

$6O_2$

_ X _ _ _ _ _ _ _ _ _

_ _ _ M _ _ _ _ _ _

_ F _ _ _ _ _ _ _ S _

$C_6H_{12}O_6$

FIND THE TWO SUBSTANCES THAT THE PLANT CELL USES TO MAKE ITS OWN FOOD!

GLUCOSE IS A SUGAR THAT PLANTS STORE TO MAINTAIN A STEADY FOOD SUPPLY.

_ _ _ N _ _ _ _ _ _

Dr. Birdley Teaches Science – Introducing Cells

NAME:_____

CLASS:_____ DATE:_____

VOCABULARY
BUILD-UP!

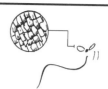

Directions: Read the definitions. Then, write sentences to convey the meaning of the underlined words.

1. <u>Cells</u> are tiny compartments that all living things are made of. They are the smallest things alive! Examples include plant cells, muscle cells, and nerve cells. Use the term <u>cell</u> in a sentence.

_____

_____

2. An <u>organ</u> is a major part of the body that performs a particular task. Examples include the heart, brain, stomach, liver, and intestines. Use the term <u>organ</u> in a sentence.

_____

_____

3. <u>Tissues</u> are organized groups of cells. The example here is <u>endothelial tissue</u>, which forms a protective inner lining within the heart's passages. Other examples include nerve and muscle tissue. Use the term <u>tissue</u> in a sentence.

_____

_____

4. <u>Photosynthesis</u> is a process by which a plant cell uses water, carbon dioxide, and sunlight to create food and oxygen gas. This process enables the plant to maintain a steady food supply. Use <u>photosynthesis</u> in a sentence.

_____

_____

5. A <u>microorganism</u> is a tiny living thing that can only be seen in detail through a microscope. Many of them are made of one cell. The two pictured are a euglenoid (left) and a paramecium (right). Use <u>microorganism</u> in a sentence.

_____

_____

Dr. Birdley Teaches Science – Introducing Cells

NAME:_____

CLASS:_____ DATE:_____

 Graphic Organizer

Support each key statement with evidence that you have learned.

Cells give living things form and function.

Cells give parts of living things their structure.

Cells perform vital tasks for the organism.

Specific cell type(s):

Specific cell process:

Tissue(s) that these cell types form:

Importance:

Organ(s) that the tissue(s) helps to form:

Cell types that carry out this process:

Dr. Birdley Teaches Science – Introducing Cells

Name:_____ Class:_____ Date:_____

Unit 1 Quiz: The Importance of Cells

Directions: This quiz tests your knowledge of the chapter's cartoon, background article, and visual exercises. Answer the following questions to the best of your ability.

1. Cells conduct photosynthesis in order to produce:
   - (a) water
   - (b) chlorophyll
   - (c) glucose
   - (d) carbon dioxide

2. The process of photosynthesis is primarily
   - (a) chemical
   - (b) electrical
   - (c) mechanical
   - (d) technological

3. Cells arrange themselves to form:
   - (a) organelles
   - (b) tissues
   - (c) molecules
   - (d) microorganisms

4. The inner lining of the heart's passageways is made up of:
   - (a) smooth muscle cells
   - (b) nerve cells
   - (c) red blood cells
   - (d) endothelial cells

5. Microorganisms are:
   - (a) living things that are often made of one cell
   - (b) parts of the cell that perform specific functions.
   - (c) cell types within the human body
   - (d) small organs made of many cells

6. Which of the following statements is false?
   - (a) all living things are made of cells
   - (b) cells are the smallest units of life
   - (c) cells form spontaneously in between other cells
   - (d) multicellular and unicellular organisms exist

7. Explain how cells, organs, and tissues are related.

   _____

   _____

   _____

   _____

Dr. Birdley Teaches Science – Introducing Cells

Unit 2: The Hierarchy of Life

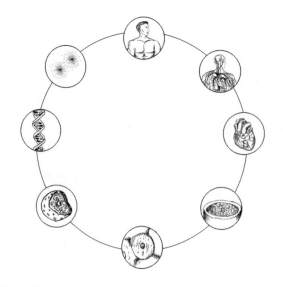

Contents

NAME:_____

CLASS:_____ DATE:_____

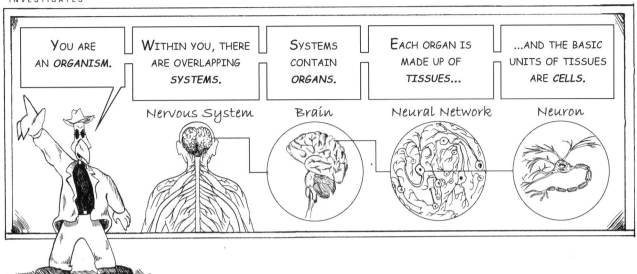

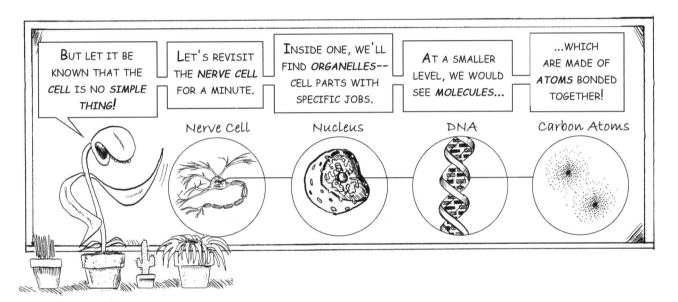

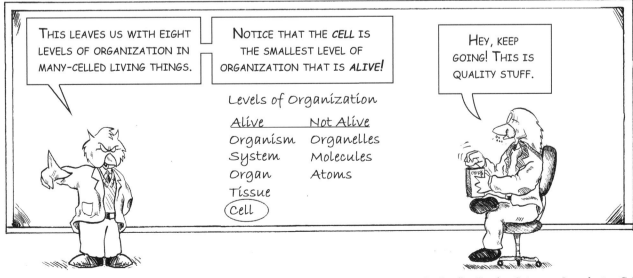

Dr. Birdley Teaches Science – Introducing Cells

Know Your Levels

Objectives

1. To illustrate eight levels of organization in multicellular living things.

2. To introduce the idea that the cell is the smallest level of organization that is still alive.

Synopsis

As Birdley takes a break, Jaykes, Phyll, and Dean Owelle discuss eight levels of organization in multicellular living things.

Main Ideas

1. Many-celled organisms have multiple levels of organization.

2. Organisms, or living things, contain overlapping systems.

3. Systems are made up of organs and supporting parts.

4. Organs are made up of tissues, which are composed of cells.

5. Cells contain organelles, which are made up of groups of molecules.

6. Molecules are made up of atoms.

Vocabulary

system	cell	molecule
organ	organelle	atom
tissue	organism	

Characters

Jaykes, Phyll the plant, Dean Owelle, Dr. Birdley

Questions for Discussion

Before Reading:

1. What are human systems made up of?

2. What are cells made up of?

After Reading:

1. Which levels are living? Which are non-living?

2. What level is the smallest unit of matter?

3. What level is the smallest unit of life?

4. What are other types of (systems, organs, tissues, etc.) that could be illustrated in the diagram?

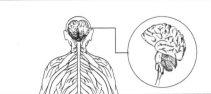

Background: Know Your Levels

Many-celled living things have multiple levels of organization, known as a hierarchy. The eight levels of organization, from largest to smallest, include organisms, systems, organs, tissues, cells, organelles, molecules, and atoms.

You, as an organism, contain overlapping systems. These systems, such as the nervous system, muscular system, and cardiovascular system, extend throughout your body. The example given is the nervous system, which controls your body's movement, learning, memory, and all other activity associated with the brain.

Systems contain at least one organ. Each organ performs a specific function. The organ in this case is the brain. Like all organs, the brain is made up of tissues, which are groups of cells. The cell occupies the smallest level of organization that is still alive. The cells pictured above are the nerve cell (top right) and the plant cell (inset).

Each cell contains cell parts, known as organelles. The organelle illustrated is the nucleus, which controls the cell. Organelles are like organs of the

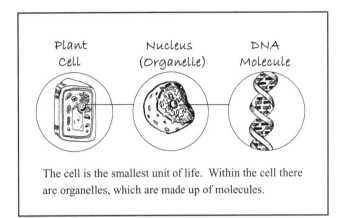

Plant Cell   Nucleus (Organelle)   DNA Molecule

The cell is the smallest unit of life. Within the cell there are organelles, which are made up of molecules.

cell because they perform specific functions. The building blocks of organelles are molecules. In this case, the molecule presented is DNA, which resides in the nucleus.

Other types of systems may also have multiple levels of organization. A school system, for example, is organized into districts, which are made up of various schools. Each school population is composed of different groups: the teachers, administrators, and students. These levels of organization, from system, to district, to school, to individuals, are analogous to those within multicellular living things.

1. List the eight levels of organization that are discussed, from smallest to largest.

_____

_____

2. How is an organ similar to an organelle?

_____

_____

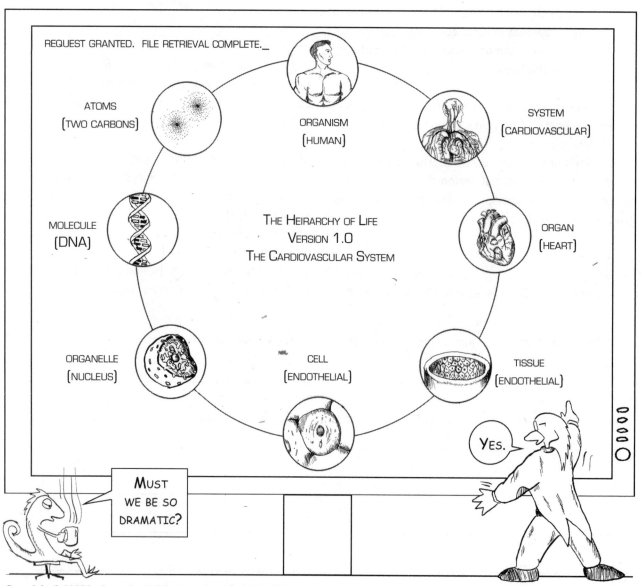

Dr. Birdley Teaches Science – Introducing Cells

NAME:_____

CLASS:_____ DATE:_____

STUDY QUESTIONS

Directions: Answer the following questions to the best of your ability.

1. What information does this cartoon provide on many-celled living things?

_____

_____

2. What two important points does the cartoon make about cells?

_____

_____

3. Identify one type of living thing that does not have all eight levels of organization. What levels does this organism **not** have?

_____

_____

4. Which levels of organization are alive? Which levels are not alive?

_____

_____

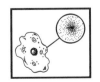

5. Compare and contrast cells with atoms. How are they similar? How are they different?

_____

_____

Dr. Birdley Teaches Science – Introducing Cells

THE HIERARCHY OF LIFE

DR. BIRDLEY
INVESTIGATES

NAME:_____

CLASS:_____ DATE:_____

GIVE EACH SPECIMEN ITS **CORRECT NAME,** AND
IDENTIFY ITS **LEVEL OF ORGANIZATION.**
USE THE TERMS FROM THE WORD BANK.

SPECIMEN NAMES	LEVELS OF ORGANIZATION
HEART	ORGAN
ENDOTHELIAL TISSUE	TISSUE
ENDOTHELIAL CELL	CELL
CARDIOVASCULAR SYSTEM	SYSTEM
DNA	MOLECULE
NUCLEUS	ORGANELLE
TWO CARBON ATOMS	ATOMS
HUMAN	ORGANISM

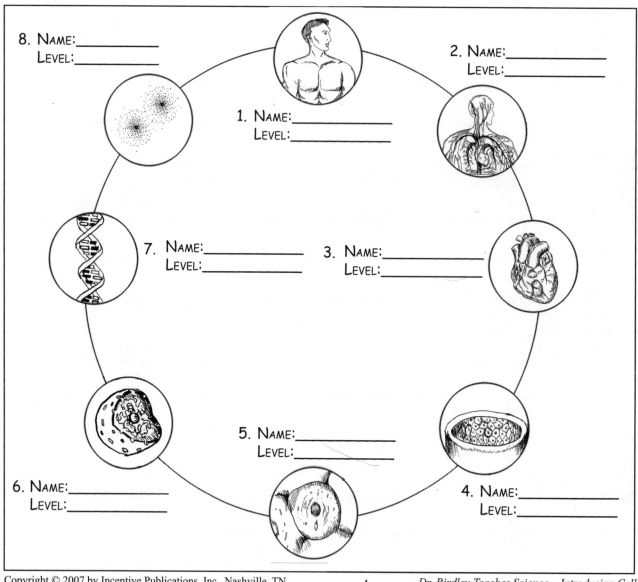

8. NAME:_____
   LEVEL:_____

1. NAME:_____
   LEVEL:_____

2. NAME:_____
   LEVEL:_____

7. NAME:_____
   LEVEL:_____

3. NAME:_____
   LEVEL:_____

6. NAME:_____
   LEVEL:_____

5. NAME:_____
   LEVEL:_____

4. NAME:_____
   LEVEL:_____

Dr. Birdley Teaches Science – Introducing Cells

VOCABULARY
BUILD-UP!

Directions: Read the definitions. Then, write sentences to convey the meaning of the underlined words.

1. An <u>organism</u> is any living thing. The major groups include animals, plants, fungi, and microorganisms. The organism pictured to the left is the aardvark. Use <u>organism</u> and <u>cells</u> in a sentence.

_____

_____

2. A <u>system</u> is a network of organs and supporting parts, usually extending throughout the body. Examples include the nervous system, cardiovascular system (left), and skeletal system. Use <u>system</u> in a sentence.

_____

_____

3. An <u>organelle</u> is a cell part that performs a specific function. One example is the nucleus (left), which stores the cell's DNA and controls the cell's other activities. Use the term <u>organelle</u> in a sentence.

_____

_____

4. A <u>molecule</u> is an organized structure, smaller than the cell, made up of atoms linked together. Examples include DNA (left), water, and carbon dioxide. Use the term <u>molecule</u> in a sentence.

_____

_____

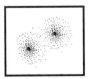

5. <u>Atoms</u> are the tiny particles that all matter is made up of. Atoms link up to form molecules. Examples include carbon, hydrogen, and oxygen atoms. Use the term <u>atom</u> in a sentence.

_____

_____

Dr. Birdley Teaches Science – Introducing Cells

NAME:_____
CLASS:_____ DATE:_____

Graphic Organizer

To the left of each definition, write the name of the level of organization that is described. To the right of the definition, give one to three examples

Level	Definition	Examples
	a living thing	
	a network of interconnected parts	
	a part of the body that serves a specific function	
	a group of cells	
	the smallest unit of life	
	a cell part that performs a specific function	
	a structure made of atoms bonded together	
	the smallest unit of matter	

Dr. Birdley Teaches Science – Introducing Cells

Name:_____Class:_____Date:_____

Unit 2 Quiz: The Hierarchy of Life

Directions: Answer the following questions to the best of your ability.

Section A: Labeling. Identify each specimen. Then, indicate whether it is a system, organ, tissue, cell, or organelle.

 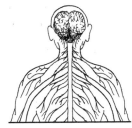   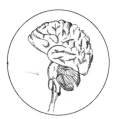

1. _____   2. _____   3. _____   4. _____   5. _____

Section B: Short Answer.

1. In the space below, explain how specimens 2, 3, 4, and 5 are related. Use the terms you listed above in your answer.

_____

_____

_____

_____

_____

2. Explain how specimens 1 and 3 are different. _____

_____

_____

Dr. Birdley Teaches Science – Introducing Cells

Unit 3: The Smallest Units of Life

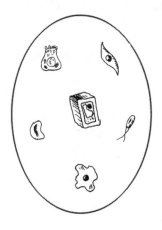

Contents

NAME:_____

CLASS:_____ DATE:_____

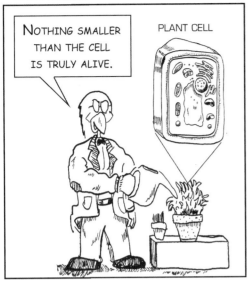

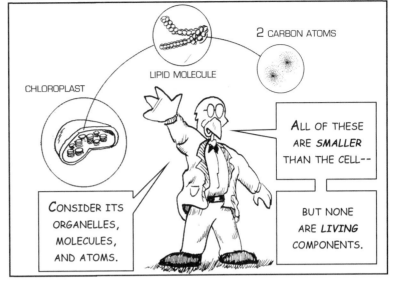

Dr. Birdley Teaches Science – Introducing Cells

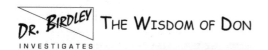

DR. BIRDLEY INVESTIGATES

THE WISDOM OF DON

NAME:_____

CLASS:_____ DATE:_____

HMM. WHAT DO CELLS *DO* THAT MAKE THEM QUALIFY AS LIVING?

THE ANSWER IS ALL AROUND YOU.

OPEN YOUR EYES, BIRDLEY. ALL THE LIVING THINGS AROUND US ARE GROWING. WHAT HAPPENS AT THE CELLULAR LEVEL THAT MAKES THEM GROW?

WAIT. DON'T TELL ME.

AH YES! CELL DIVISION.

EXACTLY.

AT THIS VERY MOMENT, THE CELLS IN THIS PLANT ARE QUIETLY COPYING THEIR DNA...

...THEN THEIR CELL BODIES *EXPAND*...

...AND THEY *REPRODUCE*, CAUSING THE PLANT TO GROW.

BECAUSE WE SEE THE PLANT *GROWING,* WE CAN INFER THAT ITS CELLS ARE *REPRODUCING*...SOMETHING ONLY LIVING THINGS CAN DO.

TRUE. BUT I DON'T SEE IT WORKING FOR A SINGLE LESSON. PLANT GROWTH IS SO SLOW, WE WOULD HAVE TO TRACK IT FOR WEEKS ON END!

WHOAH.

MUST BE GOOD SOIL.

KATZ '06

Dr. Birdley Teaches Science – Introducing Cells

Objective

1. To establish the cell as the smallest unit of life.

2. To contrast the cell with organelles, molecules, and atoms.

Synopsis

Birdley explains that cells contain organelles, molecules, and atoms. Because these items are not living, Dr. Birdley argues that cells are the smallest units of life. Nate then appears, asking him whether cells are truly alive.

Main Ideas

1. Cells contain cell parts with specific jobs, known as organelles.

2. Organelles are made up of molecules.

3. Molecules are made up of atoms bonded together.

4. Organelles, molecules, and atoms are not alive, so cells may be the smallest units of life.

5. Cells can only be alive if they show true characteristics of living things.

Vocabulary

organelle	chloroplast	membrane
molecule	lipid	bond
atom	carbon	photosynthesis

Characters

Dr. Birdley and Nate

Questions for Discussion

Before Reading:

1. What do you think is inside a cell?

2. What is the meaning behind the phrase, *smallest unit of life?*

After Reading:

1. How is a cell different from an atom?

2. What is the difference between an organ and an organelle? How are they similar?

3. What is Dr. Birdley's main point? How does he defend it?

4. What is Nate's objection?

THE WISDOM OF DON

Objective

1. To provide evidence that cells are alive by showing that they can reproduce.

2. To illustrate how cell division leads to the growth of a multicellular organism.

3. To introduce the basic stages of cell division.

Synopsis

As Birdley ponders how to prove that cells are alive, a wise pterodactyl named Don appears holding a plant. He explains how cellular reproduction causes the plant to grow, and points out that reproduction is something only living things can do.

Main Ideas

1. Because cells reproduce, they can be considered living things.

2. When they reproduce within multicellular living things, they can cause them to grow.

3. The process of cell division involves the replication of DNA, followed by the expansion of the membrane and then the division of cells.

Vocabulary

cells   growth

division   DNA

reproduction   replication

Characters

Dr. Birdley and Don

Questions for Discussion

Before Reading:

1. How is plant growth similar to animal growth?

2. What do you think the role of cells is in plant growth?

After Reading:

1. What causes plants to grow at the cellular level?

2. What evidence does this cartoon provide that cells are alive?

3. Is this enough to prove that cells are alive? Why or why not?

STUDY QUESTIONS

Directions: Answer the following questions to the best of your ability.

 1. Explain how cells and organelles are related. Which one is alive?

_____

_____

 2. Explain how organelles are related to molecules and atoms.

_____

_____

 3. Why does Dr. Birdley think cells are the smallest units of life?

_____

_____

 4. What does Nate want to know before he believes Dr. Birdley?

_____

_____

 5. Based on what you know, what are some key characteristics that cells would need to demonstrate in order to "qualify" as living?

_____

_____

Dr. Birdley Teaches Science – Introducing Cells

THE WISDOM OF DON

Name:_____
Class:_____Date:_____

STUDY QUESTIONS

Directions: Answer the following questions to the best of your ability.

1. According to Don, what causes many-celled living things to grow?

Copy

_____

_____

2. Describe the process of cell reproduction.

_____

_____

3. What argument does Don use to support the idea that cells are alive?

_____

_____

4. How is cell growth demonstrated in this comic?

_____

_____

5. What happens to the rate of cell division within the plant in the last two panels?

_____

_____

Dr. Birdley Teaches Science – Introducing Cells

 Background:
The Smallest Units of Life
The Wisdom of Don

This cartoon reinforces the point that cells are the smallest units of life, but also raises the question as to how one might prove that cells are actually alive.

Birdley points out that cells are the smallest units of life by reminding us that a cell's smaller components, the organelles, molecules, and atoms that make it up, are not alive.

The organelle in this cartoon is the chloroplast, which conducts photosynthesis for plant cells. Although the chloroplast can use water, carbon dioxide, and sunlight to produce glucose and oxygen, this does not make it alive! It would not be able to survive or reproduce without the assistance of the cell's internal "machinery."

The chloroplast's outer shell, known as the membrane, is made up of molecules known as lipids. The lipids are far simpler than the chloroplast, and show cannot grow, reproduce, or perform any other characteristics of living things. Like all molecules, the lipids themselves are made up of atoms – which are also not alive.

Birdley uses the "non-living" status of organelles, molecules, and atoms as proof that the cell is the smallest unit of life.

At this point, Nate appears and challenges Dr. Birdley on whether cells are actually living. Birdley is stumped on this matter, so Nate leaves to find the answer elsewhere.

In the second cartoon of this chapter, Birdley gets some help from a wise pterodactyl named Don, who points out that the growth of many-celled living things are caused by their cells reproducing. Because cells reproduce, he claims that cells are alive.

Directions: Answer the following questions to the best of your ability.

1. Why does Dr. Birdley feel he needs to prove that cells are alive?

_____

_____

_____

2. How does Don show Dr. Birdley that cells are alive?

_____

_____

_____

Dr. Birdley Teaches Science – Introducing Cells

DR. BIRDLEY INVESTIGATES   FROM CELLS TO ATOMS

NAME:_____

CLASS:_____ DATE:_____

FILL IN THE BLANKS WITH THE
CORRECT WORDS FROM THE WORD BANK.
YOU MAY USE EACH WORD ONCE.

- KATZ '05 -

WORD BANK

MOLECULES	BOUND
CHLOROPLAST	ASSEMBLIES
CARBON DIOXIDE	LAYERS
ORGANELLE	INWARD
ENERGY	HYDROGEN
SHELL	NITROGEN
COMBINATIONS	ELEMENTS

1. PLANT CELLS CONTAIN AN O _ G _ _ E _ _ E
CALLED THE _ HL _ R _ P _ _ S T, WHICH
CONDUCTS *PHOTOSYNTHESIS.*

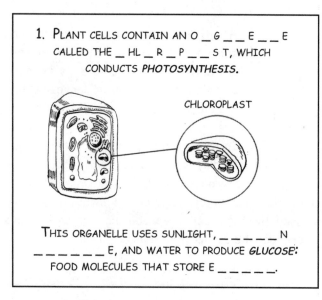

CHLOROPLAST

THIS ORGANELLE USES SUNLIGHT, _ _ _ _ _ _ N
_ _ _ _ _ _ _ E, AND WATER TO PRODUCE *GLUCOSE:*
FOOD MOLECULES THAT STORE E _ _ _ _ _ _.

2. LIKE CELLS, THE CHLOROPLAST IS ENCLOSED
BY A S _ _ _ _ L CALLED THE *MEMBRANE.* IT IS
THEREFORE A MEMBRANE–B _ _ _ _ D ORGANELLE.

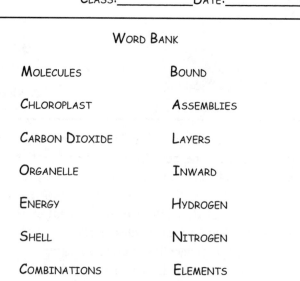

CHLOROPLAST   OUTER
                   MEMBRANE

THE MEMBRANE PROTECTS THE ORGANELLE AND ONLY
LETS CERTAIN THINGS PASS THROUGH IT.
IT IS MADE UP OF LARGE, ORGANIZED
A _ _ _ _ _ _ _ _ _ _ OF MOLECULES.

3. THE MEMBRANE IS PRIMARILY COMPOSED OF
M _ _ _ _ _ _ _ _ _ S KNOWN AS LIPIDS. A LIPID IS
MADE UP OF A HEAD AND A TAIL.

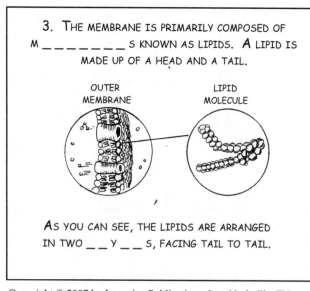

OUTER   LIPID
MEMBRANE   MOLECULE

AS YOU CAN SEE, THE LIPIDS ARE ARRANGED
IN TWO _ _ Y _ _ S, FACING TAIL TO TAIL.

4. LIKE MANY BIOLOGICAL MOLECULES, THE LIPIDS
ARE MADE UP OF FOUR TYPES OF ATOMS: CARBON,
H _ _ _ _ _ _ _ _, OXYGEN, AND N _ _ _ _ _ _ _ N.

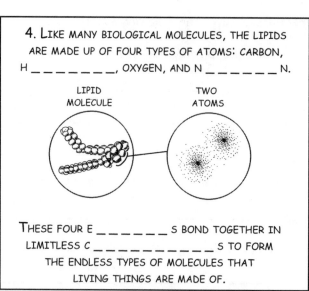

LIPID   TWO
MOLECULE   ATOMS

THESE FOUR E _ _ _ _ _ _ _ S BOND TOGETHER IN
LIMITLESS C _ _ _ _ _ _ _ _ _ _ _ S TO FORM
THE ENDLESS TYPES OF MOLECULES THAT
LIVING THINGS ARE MADE OF.

Dr. Birdley Teaches Science – Introducing Cells

NAME:_____

CLASS:_____ DATE:_____

VOCABULARY BUILD-UP!

Directions: Read the definitions. Then, write sentences to convey the meaning of the underlined words.

1. A <u>cell</u> is the smallest unit of life. Use <u>cell</u> in a sentence below.

_____

_____

2. An <u>organelle</u> is a part of a cell with a specific job. Use <u>organelle</u> and <u>cell</u> in a sentence below.

_____

_____

3. Write a definition for the term <u>alive</u>. What do you think this term means?

_____

_____

4. A <u>molecule</u> is a structure made of atoms bonded together. This particular type of molecule is called a lipid. Use <u>cell</u> and <u>molecule</u> in a sentence below:

_____

_____

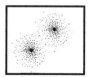

5. An <u>atom</u> is the smallest unit of matter. All the types of atoms are listed on the periodic table. Relate the terms <u>molecule</u> and <u>atom</u> in a sentence:

_____

_____

Dr. Birdley Teaches Science – Introducing Cells

Unit 4: Characteristics of Living Things

Contents

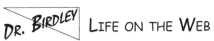
NAME:_____

CLASS:_____ DATE:_____

File   Edit   Preferences   View   Sites   Tools   Help

⬅ Back ➡   🔍 Search   ☑ Mail   ◉ Favorites

Address   http://www.prime-science.brd

Characteristics of Living Things

TRYING TO DETERMINE IF SOMETHING IS ALIVE?   ALL LIVING THINGS HAVE COMMON CHARACTERISTICS. SIX OF THEM ARE LISTED BELOW:

REPRODUCTION

LIVING THINGS CAN REPRODUCE, CREATING NEW OFFSPRING AND PASSING ON THEIR DNA.

ENERGY TRANSFER

LIVING THINGS OBTAIN ENERGY FROM THE ENVIRONMENT AND TRANSFER IT INTO A USEABLE FORM.

BEHAVIOR

LIVING THINGS DETECT AND RESPOND TO THINGS IN THE ENVIRONMENT.

ORGANIZATION

LIVING THINGS HAVE AN ORDERLY ARRANGEMENT OF PARTS.

REGULATION

LIVING THINGS CAN CONTROL WHAT GOES ON INSIDE THEM.

GROWTH

LIVING THINGS DEVELOP OVER TIME AND FOLLOW A LIFE CYCLE.

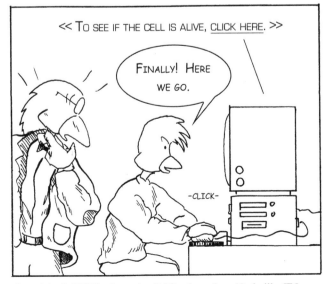

Dr. Birdley Teaches Science – Introducing Cells

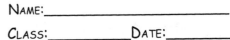
NAME:_____

CLASS:_____ DATE:_____

ORGANIZATION

SO HOW DO YOU AND OTHER CELLS SHOW ORGANIZATION?

WELL, WE HAVE AN ORDERLY ARRANGEMENT OF PARTS. EACH PART HAS A SPECIFIC JOB, OR FUNCTION.

DNA WITHIN

NUCLEUS: CELL'S CONTROL CENTER

ENERGY TRANSFER

CAN YOU OBTAIN ENERGY ON YOUR OWN?

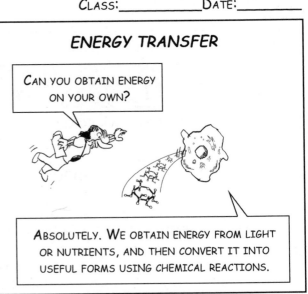

ABSOLUTELY. WE OBTAIN ENERGY FROM LIGHT OR NUTRIENTS, AND THEN CONVERT IT INTO USEFUL FORMS USING CHEMICAL REACTIONS.

REGULATION

HOW DO YOU KNOW YOU'RE OBTAINING NUTRIENTS AND NOT ABSORBING TOXINS?

I AUTOMATICALLY CONTROL THE TYPES OF SUBSTANCES I TAKE IN USING A SEMIPERMEABLE SHELL, CALLED A **MEMBRANE.**

GROWTH

HOW ABOUT GROWTH? CELLS CAN ONLY GROW SO LARGE.

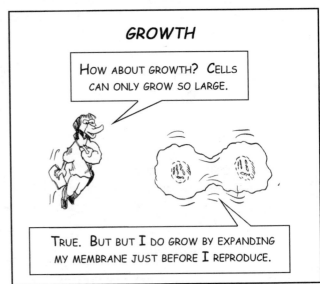

TRUE. BUT BUT I DO GROW BY EXPANDING MY MEMBRANE JUST BEFORE I REPRODUCE.

REPRODUCTION

AND BY THE WAY...

CELLS REPRODUCE BY DIVIDING IN TWO.

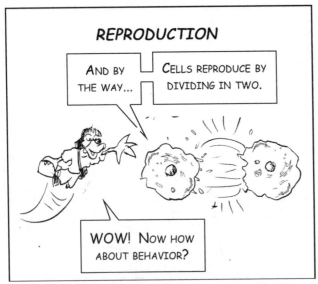
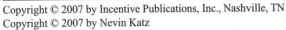

WOW! NOW HOW ABOUT BEHAVIOR?

BEHAVIOR

WE BEHAVE BY COMMUNICATING THROUGH CHEMICAL OR ELECTRICAL SIGNALS.

THANKS, GUYS!

NO PROBLEM.

Dr. Birdley Teaches Science – Introducing Cells

Objective

To define six characteristics of life.

Synopsis

To find out whether cells are alive, Nate tries to find the answer on the Internet. Before finding the answer, he runs across a Web site that defines six characteristics of life.

Main Idea

All living things demonstrate common characteristics of life.

Vocabulary

reproduction   energy transfer

behavior   organization

regulation   growth

Characters

Nate and Dr. Birdley

Teacher's Notes

This cartoon can be used more broadly within a biology course, since it defines six common characteristics of life. One thing I have found useful is that these characteristics spell an acronym that students find easy to remember (REBORG). The exercises in this section present additional characteristics that living things demonstrate.

Although this cartoon does not have study questions of its own, it works well when used with the vocabulary build-up. The "Interview with a Cell" cartoon and its related study questions also serve as a good follow-up to this one.

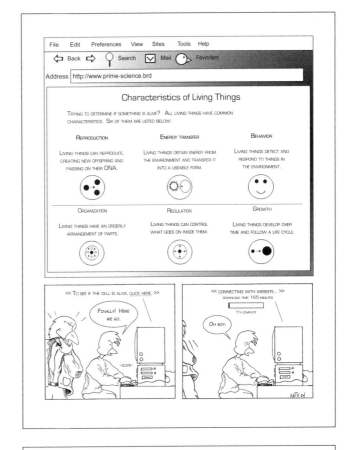

Questions for Discussion

Before Reading:

1. What characteristics do living things have in common? List as many as possible.

2. (Present students with a list of specimens.) Among these specimens, which is alive and which is not alive? Why?

After Reading:

1. How does (a given organism) show (a given characteristic)?

2. Can you explain how a cell might demonstrate (a given characteristic?)

3. What characteristics from your list were mentioned? Not mentioned?

Dr. Birdley Teaches Science – Introducing Cells

INTERVIEW WITH A CELL

DR. BIRDLEY
INVESTIGATES

Objective

To illustrate and explain how cells show six characteristics of life.

Synopsis

After using the zoom watch to shrink down to the size of a cell, Clarissa interviews a cell in order to confirm that cells are truly alive.

Main Idea

Cells can be considered living because they demonstrate six essential qualities of living things.

Vocabulary

nucleus   nutrients

membrane   cell division

regulation   growth

Characters

Clarissa Birdley (a science journalist)
and a Cell Interviewee

Teacher's Notes

This cartoon and its related study questions are designed to be used with the "Life on the Web" cartoon and its vocabulary build-up.

Although a detailed understanding of the cell membrane is not necessary, it can be useful to briefly explain how it acts as a filter for the cell.

For advanced students who have covered mitosis, it might be useful to point out that the cell would have to be going through the first several phases of mitosis in between the third and fourth panels.

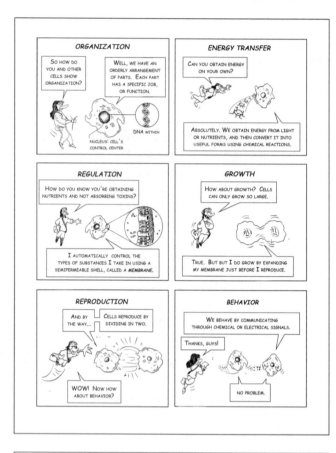

Questions for Discussion

Before Reading:

1. Do you think that cells are alive? Why or why not?

2. What characteristics of life would cells need to demonstrate in order to show that they are alive?

After Reading:

1. How did the cell demonstrate (a given characteristic?)

2. What are substances that cells need that all living things need?

3. What is the role of the nucleus in the cell?

Dr. Birdley Teaches Science – Introducing Cells

LIFE ON THE WEB

NAME:_____

CLASS:_____ DATE:_____

   VOCABULARY BUILD-UP!

Directions: Read the definitions. Then, write sentences to convey the meaning of the underlined words.

1. Energy Transfer is the ability to convert energy from one form to another. For example, muscle cells convert chemical energy into mechanical energy.

   Use energy in a sentence:_____

   _____

2. Behavior is the ability to respond to the environment, using methods such as communication or movement.

   Use behavior in a sentence:_____

   _____

3. Organization involves having an orderly arrangement of parts. In living things, many of these parts have specific functions.

   Use organization in a sentence:_____

   _____

4. Regulation in living things is the ability to control your inside systems.

   Use regulate in a sentence:_____

   _____

5. Growth is the ability to develop over time. It does not necessarily mean getting larger.

   Use growth in a sentence:_____

   _____

Dr. Birdley Teaches Science – Introducing Cells

INTERVIEW WITH A CELL

Name:_____
Class:_____Date:_____

 STUDY QUESTIONS

Directions: Answer the following questions to the best of your ability.

1. How does a cell demonstrate organization?

_____

_____

2. What types of cells would be able to use sunlight as a direct source of energy?

_____

_____

3. A cell is absorbing harmful substances. What part of the cell is not working well enough? How do you know?

_____

_____

4. How is cell growth related to reproduction?

_____

_____

5. How is communication between cells different from communication between people? How is it similar?

_____

_____

Dr. Birdley Teaches Science – Introducing Cells

NAME:_____

CLASS:_____ DATE:_____

Background:
Life on the Web
Interview with a Cell

In **Life on the Web,** Nate runs across a Web site that explains six characteristics of life.

Reproduction is defined here as creating offspring and passing genetic material (DNA) to the next generation.

Growth is defined as developing over time and following a life cycle that is directed by an organism's DNA. All living things have DNA.

Energy transfer is defined as obtaining energy from the environment and transferring it into a useful form.

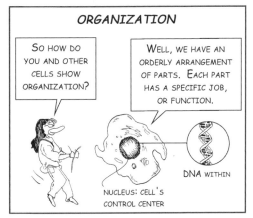

ORGANIZATION

SO HOW DO YOU AND OTHER CELLS SHOW ORGANIZATION?

WELL, WE HAVE AN ORDERLY ARRANGEMENT OF PARTS. EACH PART HAS A SPECIFIC JOB, OR FUNCTION.

DNA WITHIN

NUCLEUS: CELL'S CONTROL CENTER

Behavior is defined as detecting and responding to things in the environment.

Organization is defined as having an orderly arrangement of parts. All living things have a high degree of organization.

In **Interview with a Cell,** a miniaturized Clarissa learns how cells demonstrate these characteristics. In summary, this is what she learns:

Cells have a very organized arrangement of parts. Cells can obtain energy from nutrients or sunlight. They regulate what passes into them using their membrane. They grow by expanding their membranes just before cell division. They reproduce by dividing in two. And they communicate using chemical and electrical signals.

Regulation is defined as controlling what goes on inside a living thing. Living things control the input and output of matter and energy to create a state of balance within known as **homeostasis.**

Directions: Choose one characteristic of life. Compare and contrast how a human and a cell demonstrate the characteristic.

_____

_____

_____

_____

_____

_____

Dr. Birdley Teaches Science – Introducing Cells

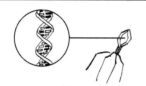 MINI-COMIC: VIRUSES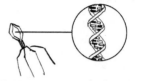

Directions: Read the cartoon and the text. Then, answer the question that follows.

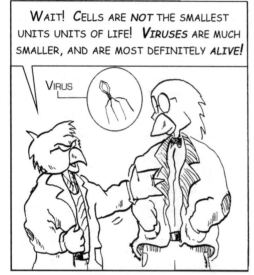

Although the subject is controversial, many do not consider viruses alive.   While cells have a rather complex interior, viruses are little more than DNA surrounded by a coat of protein.   Unlike cells and other living things, viruses are without metabolism; they do not contain the chemical reactions needed to obtain and use energy and matter.   Furthermore, they cannot reproduce on their own! They must find a host cell, and insert their DNA – the blueprint for virus assembly.   The host cell is then tricked into building new viruses using the new DNA. Because they lack complex organization, metabolism, and an independent means of reproduction, viruses do not fit the conventional definition of a living thing.

Now, build a counterargument. Why do you think some people consider viruses *alive?*

_____

_____

_____

_____

Dr. Birdley Teaches Science – Introducing Cells

IS IT ALIVE? PART 1

NAME:_____

CLASS:_____DATE:_____

WRITE WHETHER EACH SPECIMEN IS LIVING, NOT LIVING, OR ONCE LIVING. *BE SURE TO EXPLAIN WHY.* THINK ABOUT THE CHARACTERISTICS OF LIFE IN THE BOX TO THE RIGHT.

KATZ '04

CHARACTERISTICS OF LIFE	
REPRODUCTION	ADAPTATION
ENERGY TRANSFER	MADE OF CELLS
BEHAVIOR	NEED FOR WATER
ORGANIZATION	PRODUCES WASTE
REGULATION	METABOLISM
GROWTH	CONTAINS DNA

1. ONE-CELLED AMOEBA_____
_____
_____
_____

2. INSECT TRAPPED IN AMBER_____
_____
_____
_____

3. SEA ANEMONE_____
_____
_____
_____

4. COMET_____
_____
_____
_____

5. RAINDROP_____
_____
_____
_____

Dr. Birdley Teaches Science – Introducing Cells

NAME:_____
CLASS:_____DATE:_____

WRITE WHETHER EACH SUBJECT IS LIVING, NOT LIVING, OR ONCE LIVING. *BE SURE TO EXPLAIN WHY!* THINK ABOUT THE CHARACTERISTICS OF LIFE IN THE BOX TO THE LEFT.

KATI '04

CHARACTERISTICS OF LIFE

REPRODUCTION	ADAPTATION
ENERGY TRANSFER	MADE OF CELLS
BEHAVIOR	NEED FOR WATER
ORGANIZATION	PRODUCES WASTE
REGULATION	METABOLISM
GROWTH	CONTAINS DNA

1. BALLOON FILLED WITH HELIUM _____
_____
_____
_____

2. SEA STAR _____
_____
_____
_____

3. MUSHROOMS GROWING ON A LOG _____
_____
_____
_____

4. RAINCLOUD _____
_____
_____
_____

5. AN ERUPTING VOLCANO _____
_____
_____
_____

Dr. Birdley Teaches Science – Introducing Cells

DR. BIRDLEY INVESTIGATES — IS IT ALIVE? PART 3

NAME:_____

CLASS:_____ DATE:_____

> WRITE WHETHER EACH SUBJECT IS LIVING, NOT LIVING, OR ONCE LIVING. **BE SURE TO EXPLAIN WHY!** THINK ABOUT THE CHARACTERISTICS OF LIFE IN THE BOX TO THE LEFT.

KATZ '04

CHARACTERISTICS OF LIFE

REPRODUCTION	ADAPTATION
ENERGY TRANSFER	MADE OF CELLS
BEHAVIOR	NEED FOR WATER
ORGANIZATION	PRODUCES WASTE
REGULATION	METABOLISM
GROWTH	CONTAINS DNA

MUMMY_____
_____
_____
_____

CACTUS_____
_____
_____
_____

T4 BACTERIOPHAGE VIRUS_____
_____
_____
_____

EMPTY SNAIL SHELL_____
_____
_____
_____

FLAME_____
_____
_____
_____

Dr. Birdley Teaches Science – Introducing Cells

Unit 5: The Amoeba

Contents

NAME:_____

CLASS:_____ DATE:_____

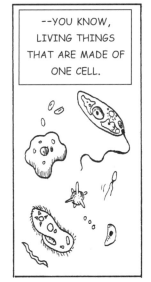

Dr. Birdley Teaches Science – Introducing Cells

THE AMOEBA

Objectives

To prove that cells are alive by showing how the amoeba demonstrates characteristics of life.

Background

As Nate scans the Internet, Dr. Birdley asks Professor Lark to help him prove that cells are alive. They decide to observe a one-celled creature known as the amoeba, which eats, moves, grows, and reproduces in an obvious manner.

Main Ideas

1. Unicellular organisms are living things made of one cell.

2. The amoeba demonstrates energy transfer by devouring and digesting a smaller bacterium.

3. The amoeba shows behavior by swimming and capturing the bacterium with its false feet.

4. The amoeba grows by expanding its membrane as it prepares to divide.

5. The amoeba reproduces by dividing in two.

Related Vocabulary

amoeba   pseudopodium (false foot)

phagocytosis   unicellular organism

Characters

Dr. Birdley, Professor Lark, and the amoeba

Questions for Discussion

Before Reading:

1. How could a microscope help you prove that cells are alive?

2. What do you already know about microorganisms?

After Reading:

1. Why is Dr. Birdley frustrated at the end of the comic?

2. What do you suppose the amoeba is doing during their "resting" phase?

3. What characteristics of life does the amoeba demonstrate? How?

Dr. Birdley Teaches Science – Introducing Cells

Background: The Amoeba

This cartoon illustrates how the amoeba shows several characteristics of life, and offers a glimpse of other unicellular organisms.

In hopes of proving to Nate that cells are alive, Birdley and Lark decide to look at unicellular organisms, because their life processes, such as behavior, are more visible than in most body cells. As Professor Lark observes the amoeba, he sees it demonstrate several characteristics of life.

In the picture shown, the amoeba extends two of its false feet (known as psuedopodia) to surround a bacterium, in order to obtain energy. The energy from the microbe, once it is digested, is transferred to the amoeba.

The amoeba shows the life process of behavior

by catching its prey in the first frame, and then swimming along using one pseudopodium.

As the amoeba swims, a bubble called a vacuole digests the amoeba's prey, and the broken down nutrients are distributed throughout the amoeba's one-celled body. The amoeba's ability to control this process is an example of regulation.

We then see the amoeba grow by expanding its membrane. In the next frame, the amoeba has reproduced by dividing in two.

This cartoon illustrates how the amoeba shows behavior, energy transfer, growth, regulation, and reproduction. Because the amoeba is made of only one cell, its actions provide evidence that cells are alive.

Directions: In your own words, list at least three reasons why we know the amoeba is alive.

_____

_____

_____

_____

_____

Dr. Birdley Teaches Science – Introducing Cells

STUDY QUESTIONS

Directions: Answer the following questions to the best of your ability.

What are unicellular organisms? Why does Lark suggest examining them?

_____

_____

2. Compare and contrast the amoeba's style of energy transfer with that of an animal.

_____

_____

3. a. Why do you think the amoeba forms the "false feet" seen in this picture?
   b. What characteristic of life is demonstrated here?

_____

_____

4. As the amoeba prepares to divide in two, its membrane expands. What characteristic of life is demonstrated in this case? Explain.

_____

_____

5. How might these findings help Birdley prove that cells ar alive?

_____

_____

Dr. Birdley Teaches Science – Introducing Cells

THE LIFE OF THE AMOEBA

NAME:_____

CLASS:_____ DATE:_____

C'MON, LARK! FILL IN THE BLANKS WTIH THE WORDS IN THE BANK!!

WORD BANK

PSEUODPODIUM	REPRODUCTION
DIVISION	BACTERIA
VACUOLE	PROTISTS
PSEUDOPODIA	CYTOPLASM
SURROUNDING	MEMBRANE
DAUGHTER CELLS	CHROMOSOMES

---

1. WHEN AN AMOEBA DETECTS PREY, IT FORMS TWO FALSE FEET, CALLED P_SeuDOPODI_A

THE FALSE FEET ARE EXTENSION OF THE AMOEBA'S C_ytoplasm_.

---

2. THE AMOEBA TRAPS ITS PREY BY S_urroundin_G IT WITH ITS TWO PSEUDOPODIA.

THE AMOEBA ENJOYS FEASTING ON B_acteria_ AND SOMETIMES SMALLER P_rotists_.

---

3. THE AMOEBA DIGESTS THE PREY IN A SPECIAL BUBBLE CALLED A V_acuole_.

MEANWHILE, THE AMOEBA MOVES BY FORMING ONE P_seudopodiu_M. IT USES THIS FOR PROPULSION.

---

4. SSSHH! THE AMOEBA IS PREPARING FOR D_ivision_ BY COPYING ITS DNA.

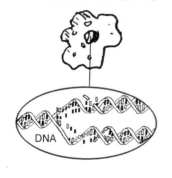

DNA

---

5. AN AMOEBA PREPARES TO DIVIDE BY EXPANDING ITS M_embrane_.

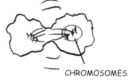

CHROMOSOMES

MEANWHILE, BUNDLES OF DNA KNOWN AS C_hromosome_S TRAVEL TO EITHER SIDE.

---

6. LOOK! THE AMOEBA HAS DIVIDED INTO TWO D_aughter cells_

EACH OF THESE CELLS HAS ONE COMPLETE COPY OF DNA. THE PROCESS OF R_eproductio_N IS COMPLETE!

Dr. Birdley Teaches Science – Introducing Cells

DR. BIRDLEY CELLS ARE ALIVE!
INVESTIGATES

IDENTIFY THE CHARACTERISTIC OF LIFE DEMONSTRATED BY EACH SPECIMEN. DEFEND YOUR ANSWER IN ONE SENTENCE.

BEHAVIOR. THE SPECIMEN IS TALKING

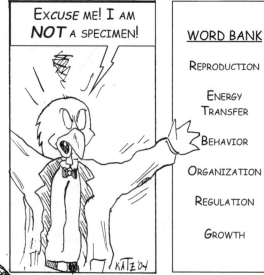

EXCUSE ME! I AM **NOT** A SPECIMEN!

WORD BANK

REPRODUCTION

ENERGY TRANSFER

BEHAVIOR

ORGANIZATION

REGULATION

GROWTH

1. THE PARAMECIUM, A ONE-CELLED CREATURE, DETECTS AND CHASES A HAPLESS BACTERIUM.

_____
_____
_____
_____

2. A BACTERIUM DIVIDES IN TWO THROUGH THE PROCESS OF BINARY FISSION.

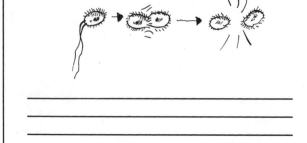

_____
_____
_____

3. THE CELL CONTAINS AN ORDERLY ARRANGEMENT OF ORGANELLES.

_____
_____
_____

4. THE MITOCHONDRION USES FOOD MOLECULES AND OXYGEN TO MAKE USEABLE FORMS OF ENERGY.

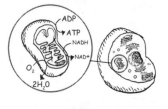

_____
_____
_____
_____

Dr. Birdley Teaches Science – Introducing Cells

DR. BIRDLEY CELLS ARE ALIVE!
INVESTIGATES

5. A T-CELL COMMUNICATES
WITH OTHER IMMUNE CELLS
ABOUT FOREIGN INVADERS.

_____
_____
_____
_____

6. A PLANT CELL ABSORBS LIGHT
PARTICLES TO PRODUCE FOOD
USING PHOTOSYNTHESIS.

_____
_____
_____
_____

7. NEURONS IN THE BRAIN COMMUNICATE
WITH EACH OTHER USING CHEMICAL
AND ELECTRICAL SIGNALS.

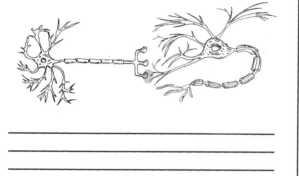

_____
_____
_____
_____

8. IN PREPARATION FOR
CELL DIVISION, THE MEMBRANE
OF A CELL EXPANDS.

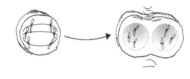

_____
_____
_____
_____

9. WHOA! THAT CELL JUST
DIVIDED IN TWO.

_____
_____
_____
_____

10. HUNGRY MACROPHAGES CHASE
DOWN BACTERIA TO ELIMINATE
THEM FROM THE BODY'S SYSTEM.

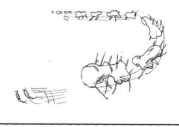

_____
_____
_____
_____

Dr. Birdley Teaches Science – Introducing Cells

THE AMOEBA

VOCABULARY
BUILD-UP!

Directions: Read the definitions. Then, write sentences to convey the meaning of the underlined words.

1. The <u>amoeba</u> is a unicellular protist that feeds on other micro-organisms. Use the word <u>amoeba</u> in a sentence.

_____

_____

2. A <u>pseudopodium</u>, which means "false foot," is an extension of the amoeba's cytoplasm. One is used for locomotion, and two are used for eating. Use <u>pseudopodium</u> in a sentence.

_____

_____

3. A <u>vacuole</u> is a bubble of digestive enzymes that break down the amoeba's prey. After the prey is digested, it circulates throughouut the body. Use <u>vacuole</u> in a sentence.

_____

_____

4. <u>Mitosis</u> is a process by which the amoeba prepares for division. During this time, DNA is sorted into two areas and the membrane expands. Use <u>mitosis</u> in a sentence.

_____

_____

5. <u>Interphase</u> is a resting stage in between divisions, where a cell builds more proteins and replicates its DNA. Use <u>interphase</u> in a sentence.

_____

_____

Dr. Birdley Teaches Science – Introducing Cells

MINI-COMIC: NATE MEETS THE AMOEBA

Directions: Read the cartoon and the text. Then, complete the exercise below.

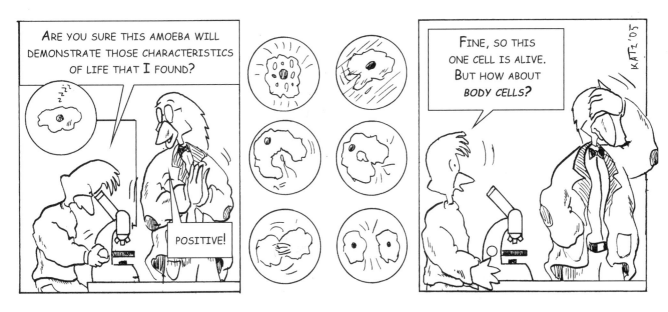

Earlier, Birdley had explained that cells were the smallest units of life. Nate's objection was that he doubted whether cells were alive. On the Web, Nate learned six characteristics of living things: reproduction, organization, energy transfer, regulation, behavior, and growth. Here, Birdley shows him that the amoeba, a one-celled organism, does demonstrate these characteristics, providing some evidence that cells are alive.

Now, explain how the amoeba demonstrates these characteristics of living things! Two are done for you.

Organization: <u>shows off its internal organelles</u>_____

Behavior:_____

Energy Transfer:_____

Regulation: <u>controls the digestion of the microbe</u>_____

Growth:_____

Reproduction:_____

Unit 6: Discovering Cells

Contents

CELL SIZE

CELLS COME IN A VARIETY OF INTERESTING SHAPES – BUT MAKE NO MISTAKE!

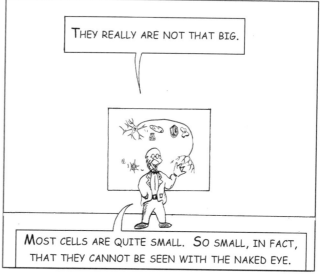

THEY REALLY ARE NOT THAT BIG.

MOST CELLS ARE QUITE SMALL. SO SMALL, IN FACT, THAT THEY CANNOT BE SEEN WITH THE NAKED EYE.

SEE THIS METRIC RULER?

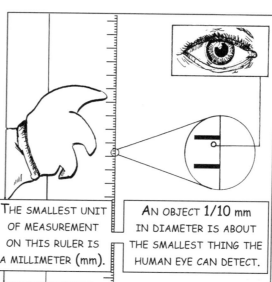

THE SMALLEST UNIT OF MEASUREMENT ON THIS RULER IS A MILLIMETER (mm).

AN OBJECT 1/10 mm IN DIAMETER IS ABOUT THE SMALLEST THING THE HUMAN EYE CAN DETECT.

MOST CELLS HAVE DIAMETERS SMALLER THAN 1/10 mm--

1/20 mm

MAKING THEM *IMPOSSIBLE* TO SEE WITH YOUR EYES ALONE.

AS A RESULT, THE FIRST HUMANS HAD NO IDEA THAT CELLS EXISTED...

NICE LEAF. BUT WHAT'S IT MADE OF?

AND HAD LITTLE TIME TO FIND OUT.

EVEN IN 1585 A.D., WHEN MANY PEOPLE WERE DOING RESPECTABLE SCIENCE, CELLS WERE STILL TOO SMALL TO BE NOTICED.

THERE MUST BE MORE TO BIOLOGY THAN JUST PLANTS AND ANIMALS!

PLEASE. THAT'S CRAZY TALK.

I DON'T BELIEVE IT, NED. WE'VE BEEN SWIMMING UNDER THEIR NOSES FOR CENTURIES, AND *STILL* NO RECOGNITION.

THEN, IN 1590, THE MICROSCOPE WAS INVENTED...

KATZ '04

AND THINGS CHANGED.

Dr. Birdley Teaches Science – Introducing Cells

HOOKED ON CELLS

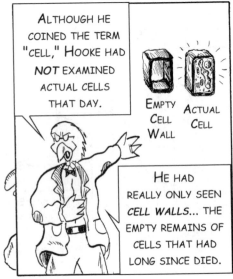

Dr. Birdley Teaches Science – Introducing Cells

CELL SIZE

Objectives

1. To give students a realistic idea of how small cells are.

2. To hint about the importance of the microscope in the discovery of cells.

Synopsis

The true size of cells is difficult to visualize. Birdley offers a point of reference by comparing the diameter of a cell to the length of a millimeter.

He also points out that cells, because of their small size, were not discovered before the invention of the microscope.

Main Ideas

1. Most cells are to small to be seen by the human eye.

2. Most cells are smaller than 1/10 millimeter.

3. Humans did not know cells existed until after the invention of the microscope.

Vocabulary

unicellular organism   millimeter

diameter

microscope

Characters

Dr. Birdley, two prehistoric people, two 16th century scientists, two microbes

Teacher's Note

Comparing millimeters to other units and practicing unit conversion are good supplementary activities for this lesson.

Questions for Discussion

Before Reading:

1. What objects are as long as a kilometer? meter? centimeter? millimeter?

2. How small do you think cells are?

After Reading:

1. How does a typical cell's diameter relate to our inability to see it?

2. Why were cells not discovered until after the invention of the microscope?

3. If you lived in the 1500s and someone had told you that cells and microorganisms existed, would believe it? Why or why not?

Dr. Birdley Teaches Science – Introducing Cells

Objectives

To illustrate how Hooke first discovered cells and coined their name.

Synopsis

Dr. Birdley tells the story of Robert Hooke, who finds that a slice of cork is made of tiny compartments. After naming the compartments cells, Hooke goes on to examine more specimens and publish his findings.

Main Ideas

1. In 1655, Robert Hooke discovered that a slice of cork was made up of tiny compartments.

2. He named these compartments cells, because they reminded him of the cells in a monastery.

3. The cork specimen actually contained cell walls, the empty remains of cells that had long since died.

4. Hooke went on to examine and draw more specimens, which included live cells.

5. He published his findings in the book, *Micrographia.*

Vocabulary

cork	compartments	monastery
cells	cell walls	*Micrographia*

Characters

Dr. Birdley, Hooke, Louis Gosling, four members of the 17th century scientific community, Louis Gosling's confidante.

Questions for Discussion

Before Reading:

1. At what point in history were cells discovered? Why do you pick this point?

2. What do you think were the first specimens that people found to be made out of cells?

After Reading:

1. What is Hooke's place in the history of science?

2. Where does the term "cell" come from?

3. How was Hooke's first specimen in the cartoon different from actual cells?

Dr. Birdley Teaches Science – Introducing Cells

NAME:_____

CLASS:_____ DATE:_____

 STUDY QUESTIONS

Directions: Answer the following questions to the best of your ability.

1. a) How are cells different?
   b) According to Dr. Birdley, what do most cells have in common?

_____

_____

2. Are humans normally able to see most cells without any equipment? Why or why not?

_____

_____

3. How do you think the invention of the microscope relates to the discovery of cells?

_____

_____

4. Explain two reasons why early humans did not discover cells. (One of the reasons is mentioned in the cartoon, but explain it in more detail.)

_____

_____

5. What are the two organisms in the cup of water? Why are they complaining?

_____

_____

Dr. Birdley Teaches Science – Introducing Cells

STUDY QUESTIONS

Directions: Answer the following questions to the best of your ability.

 1. What was the first piece of evidence Hooke found that suggested cells existed? Where did this evidence come from?

_____

_____

 2. Why was the term "cell" chosen?

_____

_____

 3. How were Hooke's initial findings different from actual cells?

_____

_____

 4. How did Hooke communicate his findings to the scientific community? If you were a biologist at this time, how would you respond to these findings?

_____

_____

 5. Discuss Hooke's microscope. Write about its importance in history, and how it is different from today's microscopes.

_____

_____

Background: Cell Size

The goal of this cartoon is to explain how small cells are relative to a millimeter, and to point out why they were not discovered until the invention of the microscope.

The Size of a Cell. Why is it normally impossible to see cells? 1/10 of a millimeter is typically the smallest size the human eye can detect. Most cells are smaller than 1/10 the size of a millimeter, or .1 mm, making them impossible to see with the unaided eye. As a result, special equipment is needed for seeing cells, such as light or electron microscopes.

Cell Diagrams. Cell diagrams in textbooks are scaled models, similar to maps. While the size of a plant cell picture may be as long as 10 centimeters (1 cm = 1×10^{-2} m) the true size would be measured in smaller units, such as nanometers (1 nm = 1×10^{-9} m).

Early Times. In early times before civilization, life

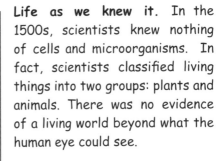

mainly involved day-to-day survival, leaving little time to investigate science. In addition, scientific methods had not been developed. The technology to develop microscopes had not come about yet. These combined factors kept humankind from discovering cells.

Life as we knew it. In the 1500s, scientists knew nothing of cells and microorganisms. In fact, scientists classified living things into two groups: plants and animals. There was no evidence of a living world beyond what the human eye could see.

Technology. The microscope was invented around 1590 by Hans and Zaccharias Janssen. This device enhanced the image size of small objects allowing the observer to see them in more detail. Although the first microscopes were not very powerful, it was only a matter of time before microscopes would allow us to discover the world of cells, forever changing the field of biology.

---

1. Explain why most cells cannot be seen with the unaided eye.

_____

_____

2. Explain why the microscope would introduce a turning point in the field of biology.

_____

_____

Dr. Birdley Teaches Science – Introducing Cells

CELL SIZE: LINKING IMAGES

NAME:_____

CLASS:_____ DATE:_____

IN THE SPACE BETWEEN EACH SET OF IMAGES, WRITE A LINKING PHRASE TO CREATE A FACTUAL SENTENCE. USE THE PHRASE BANK!

KATZ'04

PHRASE BANK

IS SMALLER THAN

WERE NOT AWARE OF THE EXISTENCE OF

CANNOT BE SEEN BY

ARE SMALLER THAN

WERE NOT DISCOVERED

WERE DISCOVERED BEFORE

UNTIL THE INVENTION OF

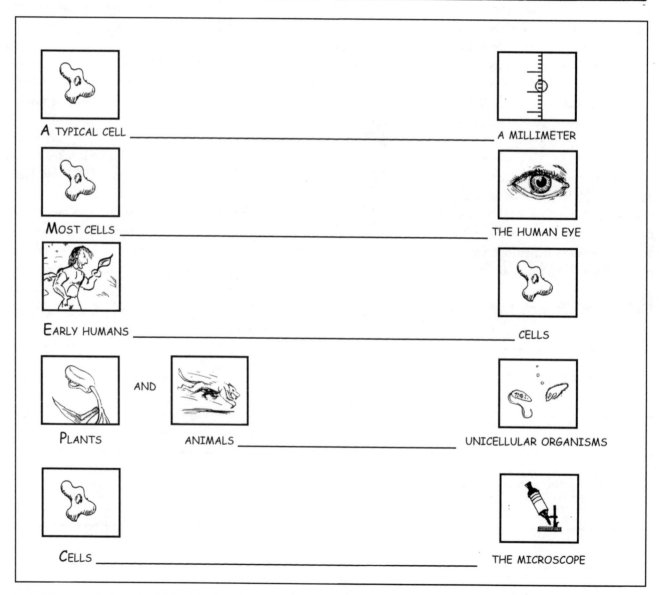

A TYPICAL CELL _____ A MILLIMETER

MOST CELLS _____ THE HUMAN EYE

EARLY HUMANS _____ CELLS

PLANTS AND ANIMALS _____ UNICELLULAR ORGANISMS

CELLS _____ THE MICROSCOPE

Dr. Birdley Teaches Science – Introducing Cells

 CELL SIZE

VOCABULARY
BUILD-UP!

Directions: Read the definitions. Then, write sentences to convey the meaning of the underlined words.

1. A millimeter is 1/1000 of a meter, and is often the smallest unit of measurement on a metric ruler. Use the word millimeter in a sentence.

_____

_____

2. Diameter is the farthest distance possible from one end of a circular object to another. Use diameter in a sentence.

_____

_____

3. A cell is the smallest unit of life. Use the words cell and size in a sentence.

_____

_____

4. A unicellular organism is a one-celled organism. These creatures were around long before we were! Use unicellular organism in a sentence.

_____

_____

5. The microscope is an invention that would eventually allow us to see cells. Use the word microscope in a sentence.

_____

_____

Dr. Birdley Teaches Science – Introducing Cells

A SMALL WORLD

THE NEXT GREAT DISCOVERY WAS WAS MADE BY A HUMBLE DRY-GOODS DEALER WITH A WILD FASCINATION FOR BUILDING MICROSCOPES: *ANTONY VAN LEEUWENHOEK!*

DELFT, HOLLAND, 1673.

LEEUWENHOEK IS AT WORK...

...FOCUSING HIS MICROSCOPE...

...EXAMINING A DROP OF RAINWATER.

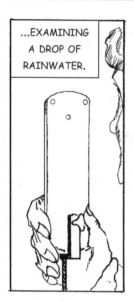

IT'S ABOUT TIME YOU FOUND US!

WHAT TOOK YOU SO LONG??

AND WHEN ARE YOU CHANGING THE WATER?

TINY CREATURES! SWIMMING AND FROLICKING ABOUT! WHERE ARE THEIR HEADS AND TAILS??

IN THAT INSTANT, LEEUWENHOEK BECAME THE FIRST TO DISCOVER ONE-CELLED ORGANISMS. OVER THE NEXT FIFTY YEARS HE WOULD FIND COUNTLESS THINGS, INCLUDING PROTISTS, BACTERIA, AND BLOOD CELLS.

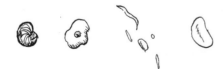

LEEUWENHOEK BECAME FAMOUS! HE WAS EVEN INDUCTED INTO THE ROYAL SOCIETY FOR HIS *MAGNIFICENT* CONTRIBUTIONS TO SCIENCE!! ARE WE SURE HE WASN'T ONE OF US??

YEP. DEFINITELY NO BEAK IN THIS PICTURE.

KATZ '04

Dr. Birdley Teaches Science – Introducing Cells

A Small World

Objectives

To portray Leeuwenhoek's initial glimpse into the world of the microbes, and highlight some of his major contributions to biology.

Synopsis

Dean Owelle tells the story of Antony Van Leeuwenhoek, a man with little formal science training who discovered the first one-celled microorganisms using his one-lens microscope.

This discovery not only helped to confirm the existence of cells, but also led him to discover additional cell types. Leeuwenhoek's research helped lay the foundations for later microbiology research.

Main Ideas

1. Leeuwenhoek lived in Delft, Holland, in 1673, where he worked as a dry goods dealer.

2. Leeuwenhoek enjoyed grinding lenses and building microscopes.

3. While examining a drop of rainwater through his microscope, Leeuwenhoek discovered one celled microorganisms.

4. Leeuwenhoek went on to discover bacteria, protists, blood cells, and sperm cells.

Vocabulary

microorganism   unicellular organism

Characters

Dean Owelle, Leeuwenhoek, Microbes, Dr. Birdley

Questions for Discussion

Before Reading:

1. What are the qualities of a great scientist?

2. Is it possible to be a scientist with little formal science training? Explain.

After Reading:

1. What was Leeuwenhoek's first major discovery?

2. From what you can see, how is his microscope different from other microscopes you have seen?

3. If you were a biologist back in his day, how might you have shaped your research in response to Leeuwenhoek's findings? Give an example.

Dr. Birdley Teaches Science – Introducing Cells

A SMALL WORLD

NAME:_____

CLASS:_____ DATE:_____

 STUDY QUESTIONS

Directions: Answer the following questions to the best of your ability.

1. What exactly did Leeuwenhoek discover? Why was it significant in the overall field of biology at that time?

_____

_____

2. Leeuwenhoek enjoyed making excellent lenses and microscopes. How do you think this activity helped him in in his scientific pursuits?

_____

_____

3. Contrast Leeuwenhoek's microscope with the traditional compound microscope Point out at least three differences.

_____

_____

4. Why do you think Leeuwnehoek was confused by the absence of heads and tails on his specimens?

_____

_____

5. How were Leeuwenhoek's other discoveries similar to each other? What conclusions or generalizations can you draw from his discoveries?

_____

_____

Dr. Birdley Teaches Science – Introducing Cells

Name:_____ Class:_____ Date:_____

Unit 6 Quiz: Discovering Cells

Directions: This quiz tests your knowledge of the chapter's cartoon, background article, and visual exercises. Answer the following questions to the best of your ability.

1. Most cells are smaller than 1/10 of a
   - (a) centimeter
   - (b) millimeter
   - (c) nanometer
   - (d) picometer

2. Cells were not discovered until after the:
   - (a) formation of the cell theory
   - (b) discovery of multicellular protists
   - (c) development of the first vaccine
   - (d) invention of the microscope

3. Robert Hooke made his first important discovery by finding
   - (a) bacteria
   - (b) blood cells
   - (c) cell walls
   - (d) nerve cells

4. Hooke made his discoveries public by:
   - (a) contacting the local radio station
   - (b) telling his neighbors
   - (c) travelling across the country
   - (d) publishing his findings

5. Antony van Leeuwenhoek is mainly known for:
   - (a) writing the first draft of the cell theory
   - (b) discovering microorganisms
   - (c) inventing the compound microscope
   - (d) preparing specimens from cork

6. Hooke's works was similar to Leeuwenhoek's because both of them:
   - (a) discovered and examined types of cells
   - (b) examined the mechanism of cell division
   - (c) worked with bacteria
   - (d) found that plant and animal cells had a nucleus

7. Explain why the discovery of cells was dependent upon advances in technology.

_____

_____

_____

_____

Review Unit: The Cell Theory

Contents

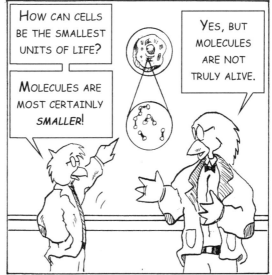

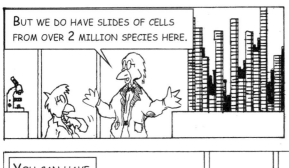

Dr. Birdley Teaches Science – Introducing Cells

THE CELL THEORY

History of Biology

Objectives

To list the three statements in the cell theory and introduce arguments that support these statements.

Synopsis

Dean Owelle challenges Dr. Birdley over the validity of the cell theory. Dr. Birdley defends the theory using reasoning and evidence.

Main Ideas

1. The cell is the smallest unit of life. Smaller parts of the cell, such as molecules, are not alive.

2. All cells come from pre-existing cells. Nobody has ever seen cells spontaneously arise out of nothing.

3. So far, it has been found that all living things are made of cells. This is supported by Birdley's slide collection, which contains cells samples from over 3 billion species.

4. Like all widely accepted theories, the cell theory is based on a great deal of evidence that has been collected over time.

Vocabulary

cells	theory	hypothesis
mitosis	fact	species
slides	opinion	tissue

Characters

Dean Owelle, Dr. Birdley, Gina

Questions for Discussion

Before Reading:

1. What is the difference between a theory and a fact? A theory and a hypothesis?

2. So far, what do all cells have in common? Try to come up with three statements.

After Reading:

1. How does Dr. Birdley finally win the argument?

2. What are the main points of the cell theory?

3. Give an example of evidence you would need to disprove the cell theory.

Dr. Birdley Teaches Science – Introducing Cells

82

BACKGROUND

A theory is different from a hypothesis because it is supported by scientific evidence The cell theory is a good example of this because although it has been revised over time, experimental findings have continued to support its central ideas.

In the 19th century, there were three scientists who helped develop the cell theory: Theodor Schwann, Mathias Schleiden, and Rudolph Virchow. In 1838, Schleiden found that every plant he examined was made of cells. In 1839, Schwann had found that all the animals he had been looking at were made of cells, and then learned of Schleiden's results.

After a great deal of research, Schwann wrote the first cell theory, which correctly stated that all living things are made of cells, and that cells are the smallest unit of life. His third statement on cell reproduction, which stated that cells formed spontaneously like crystals, was incorrect. In 1859, Rudolph Virchow revised this idea with the statement that all living things come from pre-existing cells.

Today, three more statements have been added:

· All cells contain hereditary information that is passed on during cell division.

· All cells are basically the same in terms of chemical composition.

· All energy flow of life occurs within cells.

Directions: Name at least two scientists who helped develop the cell theory. Explain their contributions.

_____

_____

_____

_____

_____

_____

Dr. Birdley Teaches Science – Introducing Cells

STUDY QUESTIONS

Directions: Answer the following questions to the best of your ability.

1. What is the cell theory?

_____

_____

2. Dr. Birdley states that molecules are not truly alive. How does this support the first statement that is discussed?

_____

_____

3. No evidence is really mentioned for the second statement of the cell theory- but explain how you could use a microscope to find evidence for it.

_____

_____

4. How does the slide collection provide evidence for the third statement in the cell theory?

_____

_____

5. Dean Owelle questions the cell theory. Do you think Dean Owelle was correct in backing down? Support your opinion.

_____

_____

Dr. Birdley Teaches Science – Introducing Cells

 EVALUATING EVIDENCE

EXAMINE THE EVIDENCE BELOW. THEN, ANSWER THE QUESTIONS THAT FOLLOW! USE THE INFO BOXES TO THE RIGHT AS A HANDY REFERENCE.

THE CELL THEORY

1. CELLS ARE THE SMALLEST UNITS OF LIFE.

2. ALL CELLS COME FROM PRE-EXISTING CELLS.

3. ALL LIVING THINGS ARE MADE UP OF CELLS.

CHARACTERISTICS OF LIFE

REPRODUCTION	ORGANIZATION
ENERGY TRANSFER	REGULATION
BEHAVIOR	GROWTH

IT HAS BEEN SHOWN THAT THE CELLS IN A LEAF CAN GROW, REPRODUCE, OBTAIN ENERGY, AND PERFORM OTHER FUNCTIONS OF LIVING THINGS.

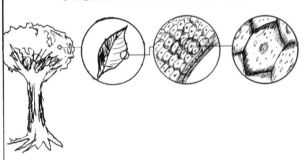

FOR EXAMPLE: PHOTOSYNTHESIS, THE PROCESS OF MAKING FOOD THAT STORES ENERGY FROM THE SUN, SUNLIGHT, IS ACTUALLY PERFORMED BY PLANT CELLS.

THE CHLOROPLAST IS THE ORGANELLE WITHIN THE PLANT CELL THAT PERFORMS THE PHOTOSYNTHESIS.

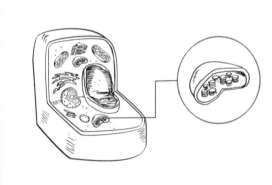

1. WHAT CONCLUSION(S) CAN YOU DRAW FROM THIS EVIDENCE?_____

_____

_____

2. WHAT STATEMENT IN THE CELL THEORY IS SUPPORTED BY THIS EVIDENCE? _____

_____

3. HOW DOES THE EVIDENCE SUPPORT THE CHOSEN STATEMENT?_____

_____

Dr. Birdley Teaches Science – Introducing Cells

THE CELL THEORY

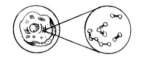 VOCABULARY
BUILD-UP!

Directions: Answer the following questions to the best of your ability.

1. A <u>theory</u> is a scientific statement (or set of statements) that is supported by a substantial amount of evidence. Use <u>theory</u> in a sentence.

_____

_____

2. A <u>hypothesis</u> is an educated guess that predicts an experimental outcome, and requires minimal evidence. Use <u>hypothesis</u> in a sentence.

_____

_____

3. A <u>fact</u> is an observation or measurement. A fact is the "what," a theory is the "why" or "how." Use <u>fact</u> in a sentence.

_____

_____

4. In the case of science, <u>evidence</u> refers to a set of experimental results that helps to support a given statement.   Use <u>evidence</u> in a sentence.

_____

_____

5. A <u>sample</u> is a specimen that comes from a larger entity. Analyzing a sample helps us to learn about the larger whole. Use <u>sample</u> in a sentence.

_____

_____

Dr. Birdley Teaches Science – Introducing Cells

NAME:_____

CLASS:_____ DATE:_____

DIRECTIONS: IN EACH WORD BALLOON, WRITE ABOUT TWO TO THREE PIECES OF EVIDENCE THAT SUPPORT THE GIVEN STATEMENT.

THE CELL IS THE SMALLEST UNIT OF LIFE! _____

_____

_____

_____

_____

_____

_____

REMEMBER! ALL CELLS COME FROM PRE-EXISTING CELLS. _____ .

_____

_____

_____

_____

_____

_____

IT'S TRUE! ALL LIVING THINGS ARE MADE OF CELLS!!_____

_____

_____

_____

_____

_____

_____

Dr. Birdley Teaches Science – Introducing Cells

CENTRAL IDEAS FROM INTRODUCING CELLS

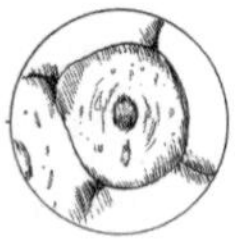

1. Cells give living things form and function.
2. Cells perform specific tasks, such as photosynthesis.
3. All living things are made of cells.
4. Systems contain central organs, which are composed of two or more types of tissues.
5. Each tissue is made up of many cells.
6. Cells contain organelles, which are cell parts that perform specific functions.
7. Organelles are made of molecules, which are in turn made up of atoms.
8. Cells are the smallest units of life.
9. Cells, like all living things, demonstrate characteristics of living things.
10. Most living things are one-celled creatures known as unicellular organisms.
11. Body cells in multicellular organisms cooperate to perform vital functions. Examples include red blood cells, cardiac muscle cells, and striated muscle cells.

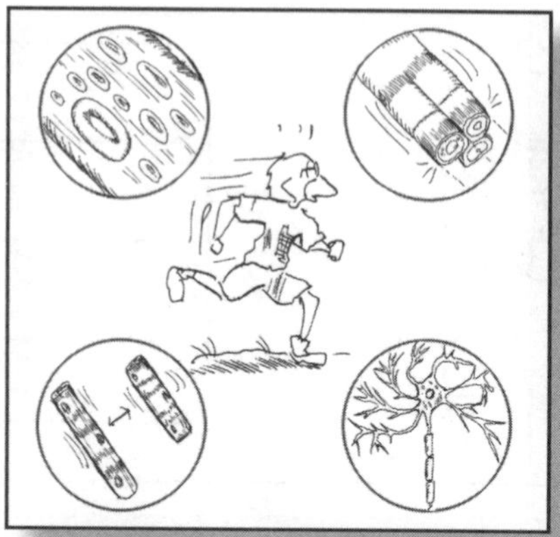

12. The amoeba, a unicellular organism, demonstrates that cells are alive by showing characteristics of living things, including energy transfer, behavior, growth, and reproduction.
13. Plants, animals, and fungi are typically multicellular organisms.
14. Protists can be either multicellular (ex. spirogyra) or unicellular (ex. dinoflagellates, amoeba)
15. Bacteria are all unicellular, and are usually smaller than protists.
16. Because most cells are too small to be seen with the naked eye, they were not discovered until after the invention of the microscope.
17. Robert Hooke discovered and coined the phrase cells, while Antony van Leeuwenhoek discovered one-celled organisms.
18. The cell theory states that cells are the smallest units of life, all cells come from pre-existing cells, and all living things are made of cells.

Name:_____ Class:_____ Date:_____

Review Quiz: Introducing Cells

Directions: Answer the following questions to the best of your ability.

1. A scientist is examining a slice of tissue under a microscope, and cannot see very much detail yet. As the magnification is increased, the first things that should be clearly identifiable are:
   - (a) molecules
   - (b) cells
   - (c) organelles
   - (d) atoms

Use the diagram below to answer question 2.

plant cell   chloroplast

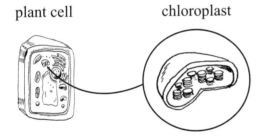

2. The chloroplast is different from the plant cell because:
   - (a) it is unable to convert radiant energy into chemical energy
   - (b) it cannot reproduce on its own
   - (c) it is unicellular
   - (d) it is able to store greater amounts of water

3. Robert Hooke coined the phrase cells while using a microscope to examine
   - (a) microorganisms in rainwater
   - (b) a blood sample
   - (c) a section of onion tissue
   - (d) a slice of cork

4. Cells combine to form _____. :
   - (a) atoms
   - (b) organelles
   - (c) tissues
   - (d) systems

Use the diagram below to answer question 5.

5. The specimens above are all examples of:
   - (a) unicellular organisms
   - (b) bacteria
   - (c) body cells
   - (d) viruses

6. Which of the following is NOT a statement of the cell theory?

   - (a) all living things are made of cells.
   - (b) cells are the smallest units of life.
   - (c) all cells are too small to be seen with the unaided eye.
   - (d) all cells come from pre-existing cells.

Dr. Birdley Teaches Science – Introducing Cells

Answer Key

Page 17: Why Cells Are Important Background Exercise

1. One example of cells performing work for the organism includes photosynthesis. In this process, cells use sunlight, carbon dioxide, and water to make food for the organism.

2. Organs are made up of tissues, which are groups of cells.

Page 18: Why Cells? Study Questions

1. Cells are important because they produce food for the plant using water, sunlight, and carbon dioxide.

2. Cells arrange themselves into tissues, which in turn organize themselves to form an organ's structure.

3. An organ is a body part made of tissues that performs a specific function. A tissue is a group of cells, and the cell is the smallest unit of life.

4. Any organism is made up of cells no matter how large or small it is.

5. Cells do work for the organism; they are the smallest units of life; they give organisms form and function; all living things are made of cells.

Page 19: Tissues of the Heart Visual Exercise – see p. 93

Page 20: Plant Cells & Photosynthesis Visual Exercise – see p. 93

Page 23: The Importance of Cells Quiz

1. c
2. a
3 b
4. d
5. a
6. c
7. Organs are made up of tissues, which are composed of cells.

Page 27: Know Your Levels Background Exercise

1. Atom, Molecule, Organelle, Cell, Tissue, Organ, System, Organism

2. Both an organ and an organelle have specific functions, and both of them are parts of something larger. (The organ is part of a system, and the organelle is part of a cell.)

Page 30: The Hierarchy of Life Visual Exercise – see p. 93

Page 32: Know Your Levels Study Questions

1. This cartoon explains that many celled living things are made of multiple levels of organization. These levels include systems, organs, tissues, and cells.

2. The cartoon explains that cells are made up of molecules and atoms, and that they are the smallest units of life.

3. A single-celled microorganism does not have these multiple levels. It is too simple to have systems, organs, and tissues.

4. The levels that are considered alive include the organism, system, organ, tissue, and cell. The levels that are not alive include the organelle, molecule, and atom.

5. Cells and atoms are similar because both are fundamental units that form larger structures. They are different because a cell is alive, whereas an atom is not.

Page 32: The Hierarchy of Life Graphic Organizer

Level, Examples
Organism, Human
System, Nervous System
Organ, Brain
Tissue, Neural Network
Cell, neuron / nerve cell
Organelle, cell part
Molecule, DNA
Atom, Carbon

Page 33: The Hierarchy of Life Quiz

Section A
1. nucleus (organelle)
2. nervous system (system)
3. nerve cell (cell)
4. nerve tissue (tissue)
5. brain (organ)

Section B

1. The nervous system contains the organ known as the brain. The brain is made up of tissues, which are groups of cells.

2. The nerve cell is the smallest unit of life in the brain, while the nucleus is a nonliving part of the nerve cell.

Page 39: The Smallest Units of Life Study Questions

1. Organelles are parts within a cell that perform specific functions. Cells are alive whereas organelles are not.

2. Organelles are made up of molecules and atoms.

3. Dr. Birdley thinks cells are the smallest units of life because their smaller components (organelles, molecules, and atoms) are not alive.

4. Nate needs to know why cells are categorized as living things in order to believe Birdley's statement.

5. Answers will vary. Some characteristics include reproduction, growth, organization, energy use, behavior, and regulation.

Page 40: The Wisdom of Don Study Questions

1. Cell division causes many-celled living things to grow.

2. The process of cell division involves the replication of DNA, expansion of the cell body, and division that produces two cells.

3. Don states that because cells reproduce, they must be alive.

4. Cell growth is demonstrated by the expansion of the cell body just before cell division.

Dr. Birdley Teaches Science – Introducing Cells

Answer Key

5. In the last two panels, the rate of cell division accelerates, because the plant grows significantly.

Page 41: The Smallest Units of Life Background Exercise

1. Birdley wants to prove that cells are alive in order to show that they are the smallest units of living things that are still living.

2. Don shows Birdley that cells are alive by showing him a plant that grows. He points out that the plant growth is due to the ability of cells to reproduce, which is a characteristic of living things.

Page 93: From Cells to Atoms Visual Exercise – see p. 93

Page 50: Interview with a Cell Study Questions

1. The cell demonstrates organization by having a highly orderly arrangement of parts with specific functions, such as the nucleus, which controls the cell.

2. Plant cells and plant-like microbes would be able to obtain energy from sunlight using the process of photosynthesis.

3. The membrane is not working well enough, because it regulates what passes into and out of the cell.

4. Cell growth involves the expansion of the membrane, which occurs just before cell division.

5. The communication between cells involves chemicals or electricity, whereas communication between people involves written and spoken languages.

Page 51: Life on the Web Background Exercise

Answers will vary, but some possible answers are listed below.

Reproduction: Whereas humans reproduce by giving birth, cells reproduce by dividing in two.

Growth: Whereas humans grow by going through a series of developmental stages, cells grow by expanding their membrane.

Organization: Whereas humans contain systems and organs, cells contain organelles.

Regulation: Whereas humans regulate properties like body temperature and blood sugar level, cells regulate the concentration of chemicals inside their membrane.

Behavior: Whereas cells follow basic drives (eating), human behavior is more complex.

Energy Transfer: Whereas humans eat and drink, cells ingest nutrients through their membrane or by engulfing it in their cytoplasm.

Page 59: The Amoeba Background Exercise

We know the amoeba is alive because of the following:
• It eats by engulfing its prey

• It reproduces by dividing in two
• It grows by expanding its membrane
• It moves using its false food (pseudopodium)

Page 60: The Amoeba Study Questions

1. A unicellular organism is a one-celled living thing. Lark recommends examining them to see if they can demonstrate life processes and help Birdley prove that cells are alive.

2. Like an animal, the amoeba must break down food to obtain energy. Instead of being broken down in a digestive system, the food gets digested within a single cell.

3. The false feet are used for propulsion. The amoeba in this case demonstrates behavior, because it is moving.

4. The amoeba demonstrates growth because the size of its membrane increases.

5. Because it is a one-celled organism, the amoeba's ability to carry out the above life processes provides evidence that cells are alive.

Page 62: Cells Are Alive 1 Visual Exercise – see p. 94

Page 63: Cells Are Alive 2 Visual Exercise – see p. 94

Page 65: Nate Meets the Amoeba Mini-Comic

Organization: shows off its internal organelles

Behavior: moves using it pseudopodium (false foot)

Energy Transfer: engulfs bacterium using two false feet (extensions of its cytoplasm)

Regulation: controls the digestion of the microbe

Growth: expands its membrane

Reproduction: divides into two cells

Page 71: Cell Size Study Questions

1. a) Cells come in a variety of shapes and sizes.

   b) However, they are similar in that most of them are too small to be seen by the human eye.

2. Humans are normally not able to see cells without equipment because they are too small to be seen with the unaided eye.

3. The microscope was necessary for the discovery of cells because it was at the time the only device that allowed humans to see objects as small as cells.

4. Early humans did not discover cells because they did not have the technology necessary to see objects that small.

5. The two organisms in the cup of water are one-celled protists (a paramecium and euglenoid, to be exact). They are complaining because after thousands of years they still have not been discovered.

Dr. Birdley Teaches Science – Introducing Cells

Answer Key

Page 72: Hooked on Cells Study Questions

1. Hooke's first piece of evidence was a slice of cork that came from the bark of a tree.

2. The term "cell" was chosen because the compartments reminded Hooke of the rooms, or cells, in a monastery.

3. Hooke found cell walls, which were the empty remains of cells that had died.

4. Hooke communicated his findings to others by publishing his work in the book *Micrographia.*

5. Hooke's microscope looks less complex, with fewer objectives and probably lower magnification. It was important because it enabled Hooke to discover cells.

Page 73: Cell Size Background Exercise

1. Cells are too small to be seen with the unaided eye because they are too small (typically smaller than 1/10 of a millimeter.)

2. The microscope would be a turning point in the field of biology because it would allow scientists to examine life at the cellular level by looking at tissues and micro-organisms. It would also ultimately lead scientists to examine the chemistry of life by exploring what cells are made of.

Page 74: Cell Size: Linking Image Visual Exercise – see p. 94

Page 78: A Small World Study Questions

1. Leeuwenhoek discovered one-celled organisms, as well as a variety of other cell types. This was significant because few cell types had been discovered at that point in history.

2. Leeuwenhoek's lenses could have been used in his microscopes, enabling him to see his specimens.

3. In contrast to the traditional compound microscope, Leeuwnehoek's microscope had one lens, it had a tip for placing specimens instead of a stage for mounting slides, and it did not have as many magnification settings.

4. Leeuwenhoek was confused about the specimens not having heads or tails because only moving living things he had seen before were animals.

5. Leeuwenhoek's additional discoveries were similar in that they all involved examining various types of cells.

Page 79: Discovering Cells Quiz

3. c
4. d
5. b
6. a
7. Advances in technology were needed for cells to be discovered because they were too small to be seen with the unaided eye. As a result, a microscope with powerful enough magnification was required for one to see them.

Page 83: The Cell Theory Background Exercise

Matthias Schleiden discovered that all plants are made of cells.

Theodor Schwann discovered that all animals were made of cells, and developed the first cell theory. (All living things are made of cells; cells are the smallest units of life; cells form spontaneously in between pre-existing cells.) His last statement was in correct.

Rudolph Virchow stated that all cells come from pre-existing cells

Page 84: The Cell Theory Study Questions

1 The cell theory is a set of well supported statements about cells. It states that cells are the smallest units of life, all cells come from pre-existing cells, and that all living things are made of cells.

2. The statement that molecules are not alive supports the idea that cells are the smallest units of life, because it supports the idea that nothing smaller than a cell is alive.

3. Using a microscope, you could examine a cell dividing into two daughter cells.

4. The slide collection shows that numerous cells samples have been taken from a range of living things, supporting the idea that all living things are made of cells.

5. Opinions will vary. For example: The cell theory is valid because it is supported by a great deal of evidence.

Page 85: Evaluating Evidence Visual Exercise – see p. 94

Page 89: Introducing Cells Review

1. b
2. b
3. d
4. c
5. a
6. c

Tissues of the Heart (p. 19)

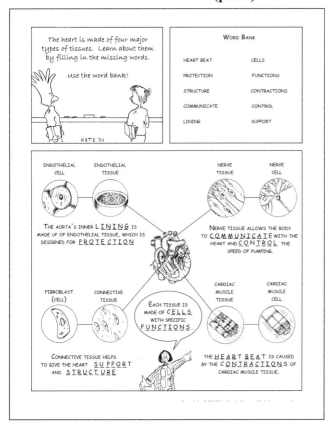

The heart is made of four major types of tissues. Learn about them by filling in the missing words.

Use the word bank!

KATZ '04

WORD BANK

HEART BEAT	CELLS
PROTECTION	FUNCTIONS
STRUCTURE	CONTRACTIONS
COMMUNICATE	CONTROL
LINING	SUPPORT

ENDOTHELIAL CELL — ENDOTHELIAL TISSUE

NERVE TISSUE — NERVE CELL

THE AORTA'S INNER L I N I N G IS MADE UP OF ENDOTHELIAL TISSUE, WHICH IS DESIGNED FOR P R O T E C T I O N.

NERVE TISSUE ALLOWS THE BODY TO C O M M U N I C A T E WITH THE HEART AND C O N T R O L THE SPEED OF PUMPING.

FIBROBLAST (CELL) — CONNECTIVE TISSUE

EACH TISSUE IS MADE OF C E L L S WITH SPECIFIC F U N C T I O N S.

CARDIAC MUSCLE TISSUE — CARDIAC MUSCLE CELL

CONNECTIVE TISSUE HELPS TO GIVE THE HEART S U P P O R T AND S T R U C T U R E

THE H E A R T B E A T IS CAUSED BY THE C O N T R A C T I O N S OF CARDIAC MUSCLE TISSUE.

Plant Cells & Photosynthesis (p. 20)

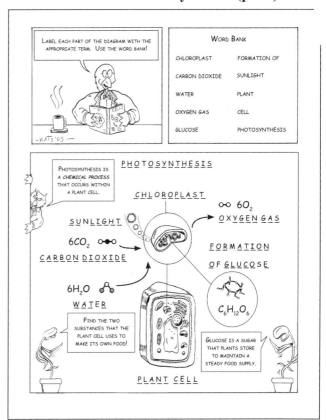

LABEL EACH PART OF THE DIAGRAM WITH THE APPROPRIATE TERM. USE THE WORD BANK!

~ KATZ '05 ~

WORD BANK

CHLOROPLAST	FORMATION OF
CARBON DIOXIDE	SUNLIGHT
WATER	PLANT
OXYGEN GAS	CELL
GLUCOSE	PHOTOSYNTHESIS

PHOTOSYNTHESIS IS A *CHEMICAL PROCESS* THAT OCCURS WITHIN A PLANT CELL.

P H O T O S Y N T H E S I S

C H L O R O P L A S T

S U N L I G H T

$6CO_2$

C A R B O N D I O X I D E

$6H_2O$

W A T E R

FIND THE TWO SUBSTANCES THAT THE PLANT CELL USES TO MAKE ITS OWN FOOD!

$6O_2$

O X Y G E N G A S

F O R M A T I O N

O F G L U C O S E

$C_6H_{12}O_6$

GLUCOSE IS A SUGAR THAT PLANTS STORE TO MAINTAIN A STEADY FOOD SUPPLY.

P L A N T C E L L

The Hierarchy of Life (p. 30)

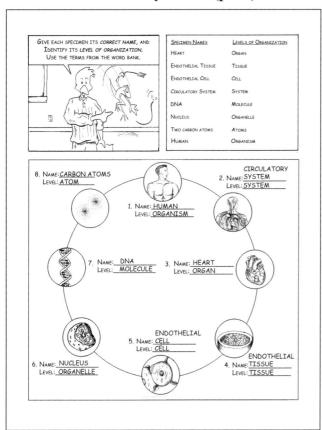

GIVE EACH SPECIMEN ITS *CORRECT NAME*, AND IDENTIFY ITS *LEVEL OF ORGANIZATION*. USE THE TERMS FROM THE WORD BANK.

SPECIMEN NAMES	LEVELS OF ORGANIZATION
HEART	ORGAN
ENDOTHELIAL TISSUE	TISSUE
ENDOTHELIAL CELL	CELL
CIRCULATORY SYSTEM	SYSTEM
DNA	MOLECULE
NUCLEUS	ORGANELLE
TWO CARBON ATOMS	ATOMS
HUMAN	ORGANISM

8. NAME: CARBON ATOMS
LEVEL: ATOM

CIRCULATORY
2. NAME: SYSTEM
LEVEL: SYSTEM

1. NAME: HUMAN
LEVEL: ORGANISM

7. NAME: DNA
LEVEL: MOLECULE

3. NAME: HEART
LEVEL: ORGAN

ENDOTHELIAL
5. NAME: CELL
LEVEL: CELL

6. NAME: NUCLEUS
LEVEL: ORGANELLE

ENDOTHELIAL
4. NAME: TISSUE
LEVEL: TISSUE

From Cells to Atoms (p. 42)

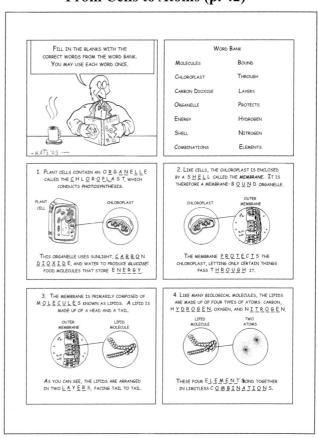

FILL IN THE BLANKS WITH THE CORRECT WORDS FROM THE WORD BANK. YOU MAY USE EACH WORD ONCE.

~ KATZ '05 ~

WORD BANK

MOLECULES	BOUND
CHLOROPLAST	THROUGH
CARBON DIOXIDE	LAYERS
ORGANELLE	PROTECTS
ENERGY	HYDROGEN
SHELL	NITROGEN
COMBINATIONS	ELEMENTS

1. PLANT CELLS CONTAIN AN O R G A N E L L E CALLED THE C H L O R O P L A S T, WHICH CONDUCTS *PHOTOSYNTHESIS*.

PLANT CELL — CHLOROPLAST

THIS ORGANELLE USES SUNLIGHT, C A R B O N D I O X I D E, AND WATER TO PRODUCE *GLUCOSE*: FOOD MOLECULES THAT STORE E N E R G Y.

2. LIKE CELLS, THE CHLOROPLAST IS ENCLOSED BY A S H E L L CALLED THE *MEMBRANE*. IT IS THEREFORE A MEMBRANE- B O U N D ORGANELLE.

CHLOROPLAST — OUTER MEMBRANE

THE MEMBRANE P R O T E C T S THE CHLOROPLAST, LETTING ONLY CERTAIN THINGS PASS T H R O U G H IT.

3. THE MEMBRANE IS PRIMARILY COMPOSED OF M O L E C U L E S KNOWN AS LIPIDS. A LIPID IS MADE UP OF A HEAD AND A TAIL.

OUTER MEMBRANE — LIPID MOLECULE

AS YOU CAN SEE, THE LIPIDS ARE ARRANGED IN TWO L A Y E R S, FACING TAIL TO TAIL.

4. LIKE MANY BIOLOGICAL MOLECULES, THE LIPIDS ARE MADE UP OF FOUR TYPES OF ATOMS: CARBON, H Y D R O G E N, OXYGEN, AND N I T R O G E N.

LIPID MOLECULE — TWO ATOMS

THESE FOUR E L E M E N T S BOND TOGETHER IN LIMITLESS C O M B I N A T I O N S.

Dr. Birdley Teaches Science – Introducing Cells

93